GUDRÚN G. BERGMANN

THE VIKING CARDS

-HERITAGE OF THE NORTH-

ILLUSTRATED BY

ÓLAFUR G. GUDLAUGSSON

EDITED BY

VICTORIA CRIBB

Library of Congress Number: 95-061765

ISBN 0-88079-783-5

99 10 9 8 7 6 5 4 3 2 1

Printed in USA

U.S. GAMES SYSTEMS, INC.
179 Ludlow Street
Stamford, CT 06902 USA

First published in Iceland in 1993 by Betra Líf Publishing.

TABLE OF CONTENTS

THE VIKING CARDS

Searching for spiritual growth, I have often traveled to foreign countries, and for a while I believed that the only true spiritual path was to be found abroad, and through cultures other than my own. My search took me deep into the spiritual traditions and shamanism of Native Americans, especially the Lakota people, with whom I fasted at Bear Butte in South Dakota while seeking a vision. But as I got to know their spiritual ways better, I felt they corresponded to the spirituality and culture of the Vikings, the first settlers of my very own country.

With this in mind, I started reading the *Sagas* of the Icelanders again. This time, I was looking for more information and knowledge about the spiritual ways of my forefathers, who settled in Iceland late in the ninth century. As my knowledge of their spiritual ways grew, the correspondence to the Native American traditions for which I sought became more evident. I discovered that, as in the Native tradition, there was no separation between the spiritual and daily life of the Vikings. They lived a life filled with spirituality and ceremonies, and offerings and prayers were part of everything they did. An element in the Viking's spiritual practice was *útiseta,* or questing for a vision. The word '*útiseta*' literally means 'sitting outside,' referring to a time spent in solitude among nature. The purpose of the *útiseta* was to communicate with the Gods, a communication that might come in the form of a vision or some inner wisdom that would be of service in the life of the quester. Like most Native Americans, the Vikings also had *godar,* or priest-chieftains, who were holy men and served as mediators between Gods and men. The godar were shamans, as they had to be able to communicate regularly with the spirit world.

In a sense the Vikings were also nomads, like many of the Native American tribes that lived on the plains. The Vikings used the summertime for hunting and traveling far and wide in their ships, trading and making friends or enemies. They met at great summer councils, competed in sports, arranged marriages, traded, and settled their disputes. During winter they usually stayed in one place, hunted in the nearby areas, and worked their skins and carved bones.

As with most of the nations that we now call primitive, the Vikings believed that all things in the world had a consciousness, and that by getting in touch with that consciousness one could seek assistance from the spirits of nature, the spirits of the ocean, the tree spirits, and the spirits of the weather and the winds. When the Vikings cultivated the Earth, they communicated with her by calling upon her spirits and the Gods of fertility. Before they set out to sea, they called upon the spirits of the ocean and the winds for safe travel, and celebrated the cycles of the Sun. The celebrations around the rekindling of the Light at the Winter Solstice (Yule; still called *jól* in Icelandic and pronounced similar to 'Yule') were without doubt the most important ones to a people who lived as far north on the globe as the Vikings did. But they also held celebrations at the Spring and Autumn Equinoxes, and the Summer Solstice called for big celebrations and festive ceremonies linked to the worship of the pagan Gods.

The Vikings were one with nature, appreciating her power and abundance, and through their spiritual practice they sought harmony with her. They believed nature provided them with guardian spirits that resided in hills and mountains, and that in some instances these guardian spirits reigned over large areas of land or even large sections of Iceland itself. Those who looked for personal protection from the spirit world communicated with guardian spirits from the animal kingdom. The animal spirits guided the Vikings and provided them with strength and endurance at critical times in their lives. The Vikings knew how to use the medicinal plants of nature for healing, and when they settled on new shores they soon learned about the medicinal plants that could be found there. They did not fear death, because it was part of their life cycle and reminded them of the eternal spiraling of all things. Nature was their ally, providing them with the means to survive, but at the same time she had their full respect. They did not try to control or reign over nature, but cooperated with her.

The daily life of the Vikings was rich in shamanism. Some individuals were born with the strong intuitive abilities of a shaman, others developed them at later stages of their lives, but all went through some form of training by the Elders. After training the men were sometimes called *vitki,* which means 'the wise one.' The women, on the other hand, were called *völvur,* which refers to the fact that some of them used sheep knuckle bones *(völur)* in their shamanic practices. Both shamans and shamanesses served the group they lived with, and their service took on many forms. Sometimes it was in the form of a spiritual healing; at other times they were sought out to foretell the future, the outcome of a battle or the prosperity of a marriage. At times their shamanic practices were used in negative ways, and some were led astray into believing they could control destiny through their skills.

If, as a spiritual Viking, you seek to train to be a shaman, please keep in mind that what you send out always comes back magnified to you, so I suggest you work with positive energy in your shamanic practice. *Ódinn,* the Creator God and Father of All, was not only the supreme God in the pagan hierarchy, but also the wisest and highest ranking of all shamans. It is therefore likely that he was worshipped by most practicing shamans, as well as by many other Vikings.

The core of shamanism, wherever it is practiced, is the spiritual experience the seeker receives through his or her everyday practice and through *útiseta.* The preparation for such an *útiseta* almost always requires fasting and a purification ritual. In some places in the world, self-sacrifice is still practiced in the form of physical exertion, as in the case of Ódinn when he wounded himself 'to death' (sacrificing of the self to the self) with his own spear while he hung from the sacred tree of life, *Yggdrasill,* for nine days and nights. (This resembles the sacrifice many Lakotas make when they fast or dance the Sun Dance.) The duration of each *útiseta* can be one or more days. While seeking this spiritual experience, the seeker often dances, drums or chants. Thus he journeys through his subconscious mind which opens up the non-ordinary realities for him, and through his vision or journey he gains a spiritual experience that creates fulfillment in his life. The old part of the individual 'dies' and the new experience represents 'rebirth' on his path of spiritual growth. Vision quests and shamanic ceremonies are usually conducted under the guidance of an experienced shaman and can be looked upon as initiations on the path of each individual's spiritual growth.

Through shamanism, one is not encouraged to worship nature, but rather learn to journey and make contact with nature and other realities, and learn to respect each of these realities. In the course of time, the connection humans once had with the non-ordinary realities and the spirit world has disappeared as societies have become more 'civilized,' and modern-day man has almost completely lost contact with them. Most of those that are now working toward greater spiritual growth wish to revive this connection with nature. Through such a revival they expect to deepen their spiritual riches, and at the same time gain a stronger connection to 'all that is,' the Creator. An ever-increasing number of people realize that without a connection to their surrounding nature and without respect for all of her realities, we cannot survive on this Earth. The Earth can survive without us, but we cannot survive without her.

Opinions differ as to the origin of the word 'shaman,' which in Icelandic is *seidmadur*. Some say it comes from the Sanskrit word *srama* which means 'spiritual experience,' but others trace its origin to the Tungus tribe of Siberia, where the word is linked to dancing and movement. It is certain that the Vikings used both *útiseta* (vision quests) and shamanic journeys when seeking a spiritual experience. In both cases chanting, drumming and dancing aided the seeker in reaching non-ordinary realities.

The idea has often been put forward, further confirmed by information recently channeled by José and Lena Stevens (both American Michael channels), that before the actual settlement took place, Iceland was a place used for shamanic training. The land is located on the boundaries of the American and the Eurasian continental plates. As hot fluid lava pushes up from the center of the Earth, the plates are pressed apart. A crack runs across the whole island from the northeast to the southwest, and Iceland has always been a place of much volcanic activity and the occasional earthquake. These activities not only release a lot of geological energy, but also mental and spiritual energy. It is believed that the shamans of the past sought out this energy, and finding it here, established the island as a training ground where shamanism flourished. People were trained in the transformation of the mind, and in journeying to non-ordinary realities. Here they sought the spiritual experience and the increased intuitive skills provided them through the solitude and challenge of surviving in the natural environment. Close contact with nature was a part of the shamanic training, and through that contact they strengthened the ties with their power animals. Some shamans could even transform themselves into their power animals.

Recharged with energy and mystical powers, the shamans returned from their training to their homelands in the northern part of Europe, and brought news of this island in the north that radiated clear energy from glaciers and active volcanoes. The Vikings were therefore not heading totally into the unknown when they set their course for the island upon which they intended to settle.

Many of the Vikings sought advice from shamans before they embarked upon the long voyage. Most of them received clear information as to where they would settle on the island, which was to be called Iceland. When they were within sight of Iceland, they threw their Totem Poles overboard, trusting they would drift ashore where the Gods wanted them to settle and where the shamans had prophesied they would settle.

Available documentation indicates that the Vikings practiced shamanism in Iceland long after the nation converted to Christianity. In the historic year of 1000, the emissary of the Norwegian king requested at the *Althing* (Council of All) that the people of Iceland should convert to

Christianity, causing a great dispute as there were many who opposed the new faith. The task of settling the dispute and seeking a peaceful solution was left in the hands of *Thorgeir Ljósvetningagodi* (the priest-chieftain of *Ljósavatn*) who was the law-sayer (*lögsögumadur*) at *Althing*. While pursuing a solution, Thorgeir relied on his abilities as a shaman, covering himself with a robe of skins while seeking spiritual guidance to resolve the matter. His decision that the Icelanders should convert to the new faith (although they were allowed to worship their pagan Gods in private) was therefore part of the shamanic tradition practiced by the priest-chieftains, who were mediators between Gods and men, and keepers of judicial and legislative powers.

Although shamanism became less apparent in everyday life in Iceland after the natives had converted to Christianity, it seems to have always been present. It was as if shamanism lived on in the soul of the nation, generation after generation, and has been preserved in the consciousness of the land. The geographical position and isolation of Iceland demanded that the people form a strong relationship with nature, and they relied on their intuition in communicating with her, just as shamans must do. A close contact with and understanding of the forces of nature, the ocean, the eruptions and other violent movements of the Earth, and the ability to read the signs of changing weather or winds, were all aspects of daily life. Being aware and intuitively open was the only way to survive. Dreams and psychic experiences guided people through their tough existence.

When the Christian faith began to get the upper hand in Iceland, most people stopped referring to the guardian spirits in nature (although Iceland's coat of arms today depicts the old pagan guardian spirits of the four directions), and instead started to use terms such as the hidden people (*huldufólk*), elves and fairies (*álfar*), dwarves and giants. These terms had previously been used, but now they signified the beings from spiritual or non-ordinary reality that made contact with the humans. All of these hidden entities are alive in the soul of the nation, and documented folklore testifies to this. The connection with beings in other dimensions still exists today and manifests itself in the respect Icelanders show the dwellings of elves all over the country. Icelanders are probably the only nation in the world where the city planning and development authorities have mapped elf dwellings.

My American friend, Patrice Noli, who is a channel and has visited Iceland several times, was once asked in her homeland whether Iceland was inhabited by spiritual people. She replied, "A nation that moves the location of its highways in order not to go through elf dwellings has to be a spiritual nation."

Icelanders have always been great story writers, and wrote their own *Sagas* during the Middle Ages. The old Sagas also covered the history of the Norwegian kings, among others. They also wrote the *Eddas,* the world's greatest and only documentation of their ancient mythology and pagan beliefs. But by the time the Eddas were written, quite a lot of information about shamanism, ceremonies and the conduct of worship had already been lost, as the natives had been Christian for about two centuries and paganism was described from the viewpoint of Christians. Therefore it was necessary for me to read between the lines and rely upon my own knowledge of shamanism when looking for information about the spirituality and shamanic practices of my forefathers the Vikings.

In creating the Viking Cards, I chose to use symbols from the everyday and spiritual life of the Vikings, and then transfer their symbolic interpretation to the world of today. The symbols that I chose come from some of the theoretical knowledge the world has of the Viking times. My interpretation of each symbol is, however, purely built on my own intuition and on material retrieved through my shamanic journeys.

My belief is that we all possess the ability to restore, in modern-day form, the shamanism practiced by the Vikings, and through that restoration gain a greater spiritual awareness. Shamanism is a simple approach to expanding your awareness as you travel through the inner worlds. In the inner worlds we can travel back and forth in time, acquiring guidance for our own life and that of others, and practicing spiritual healing. Everything originates in the spiritual world and then transforms into matter. Therefore, the origin of our own healing, the healing of the planet and our changed lifestyles is also in the world of spirit, and to make contact with that world we must practice spirituality. One way to access the spirit world is through shamanic practice. I do not see shamanism as a religion, although it is practiced within many religions, but rather as a form of spiritual practice. Shamanism teaches us respect for all those who inhabit the Earth (regardless of skin-color, race, religion, human, animal, plant or mineral form), and encourages us to gain greater awareness and make spiritual contact with those who share the planet with us, and with the Earth herself.

The Viking Cards are my contribution to the restoration of Icelandic shamanism and spirituality. I originally started working on the cards more than three years ago, but at that time I was too tied up with other things to continue my work and had to put them aside. Since that time, the Viking Cards craved many times to be 'born.' When I was finally ready to start working on them again early in 1993, and intended to pull out the first draft I had made, it was nowhere to be found.

Therefore, I started my creation of the Viking Cards anew, early one morning in February 1993. By the end of the day, I had made rough sketches of thirty-two cards. With his great artistic skills, Ólafur Gunnar Gudlaugsson transformed these sketches into beautiful drawings. When you add up three and two the outcome is five, a number that I love. According to my interpretation it symbolizes the seeking individual who desires to become a free and complete human being, and who grows through challenges and changes in his life. Great changes are often accompanied by insecurity, and at such times we need support. The Viking Cards are created to help you and me through the changes that we inevitably need to make as we transform ourselves on our path of spiritual growth.

My cards are dedicated to Ódinn, the supreme one-eyed poetic God and warrior, who was also the shaman of shamans. We call upon his powers to seek spiritual inspiration and strength when we go Viking in the uncharted territories of the inner worlds, the territories through which our spiritual growth takes us.

My name is Gudrún, and the name is made up of two words: *Gud* (meaning God) and *rún* (meaning rune). As Ódinn discovered the sacred runes, I feel my name connects me with his powers. I assume that in pagan times the name was *Godrún* ('God' being the ancient way of spelling the word for the heathen Gods). The spelling was changed and adapted when Iceland converted to Christianity. In a book on Icelandic names, my name is interpreted as 'the secret of God.'

The back of each card shows Ódinn in armor, riding his horse off to battle. In my mind he is riding to fight the battle of life itself, a battle we sometimes feel is relentless and not always victorious. Accompanying him are his ravens, *Huginn* and *Muninn.* Huginn represents the logical mind (thought), and Muninn, memory or as I like to interpret it, the intuitive mind; both represent elements of aid that we constantly use. It was the most profound wish of all my forefathers, the Viking warriors, that they would die in battle so they could dwell after death in *Valhöll* with Ódinn, where they fought battles during the day and feasted at night. Our dream, as Spiritual Vikings of the present, can be to gain strength from Ódinn to enable us to fight the 'battles' of everyday life and learn to be happy at the end of each day, grateful for yet another day in our life in which we have successfully struggled to become better. Whether we are victorious or not, each struggle brings us one step forward on our path of spiritual growth. We make the greatest progress when we stop separating our spiritual life from our physical one and learn to combine the two in everything we do.

My forefathers called it to *Go Viking* when they embarked on their adventurous journeys that led them to unknown shores where they made either peaceful or violent contact with other people. I encourage you to use your shamanic and spiritual powers and go Viking in the inner realms of your reality where you travel through the only territories in which you are completely on your own, seeking through your mind to connect with the soul and the Higher Self. Your greatest guides on your path of spiritual growth will be your five senses: taste, smell, touch, sight and hearing. You will need to learn how to use them in both the inner and outer realms of reality. Through these senses you learn to master your own life, and as you take charge of your life, your outer reality changes and develops a spiritual radiance that reflects upon your environment.

Everything in the Universe is held together by energy, Love being the most powerful of all. It is up to you whether you use the energy you possess in a positive or a negative way. Therefore, you need to read both the positive and negative applications of the energy accompanying each card in the Viking Cards deck. Having read them, it is up to you to find out which energy you are expressing in your own life. It can be either one or the other, or it can be a little bit of both. But however you express the energy, it is up to you to change it, if need be, just as everything else in your life is up to you.

My hope is that the Viking Cards may assist you, as a Spiritual Viking, on your path of growth. May you be successful as you go Viking!

Gudrún G. Bergmann

HOW TO USE THE VIKING CARDS

The Vikings were the explorers of their times, and through daring and venture they traveled and discovered new territories that were previously unknown to them. Today, all territories of the Earth have been explored, charted and settled. The only unexplored territories are those of the inner worlds, the mind and the spirit within each individual.

The Viking Cards are designed for the Spiritual Viking, the explorer of today, who undertakes the adventurous assignment of seeking settlement in the inner realms of reality in the search for greater spiritual growth. Through the cards you are also introduced to the shamanic and spiritual practice of the Vikings, as the author experiences them. By using the Viking Cards, you are not only activating your own intuitive mind and receiving guidance in your life, but also learning how to communicate with and develop respect for the consciousness of all things in your environment. The cards guide you as you seek connection with 'all that is,' the Creator, the Great Spirit, or whatever else you choose to call that Higher Power, for I believe there is but one.

How can you best make use of the Viking Cards? The cards are first and foremost a tool to help you grow. When you are distressed, undecided and feeling as if there is no way out, shuffle your deck and pull out a card. One card will do, but you can also use the following spreads which are designed to answer certain types of questions. There is no limit to the questions you can ask. Ask away and the cards will give you an indication of the energy associated with the question you are asking. Although the following spreads suggest certain ways of using the Viking Cards, you can also use them with spreads taught for other types of divination cards.

THE GUIDANCE OF ÓDINN

Ódinn was the supreme pagan *god* (old Icelandic word for God), and men called upon his powers at critical times in their lives, such as when they went into battle. But Ódinn was also the god of wisdom and protector of the poetic language, and when men wanted to be creative they called upon these powers. Furthermore, Ódinn was the master of all shamans, and his transformative powers and adaptability helped him through diverse tests of endurance. He could transform himself into many different forms and travel interdimensionally at will. When we seek the guidance of Ódinn, we are connecting with and calling upon any one or all of these powers.

Ódinn guides you through a single card that you pull from the deck. Shuffle the cards, spread them out in your hand or on a table. Form the question in your mind or ask it out loud, and pull out one card. You will find the answer to your question in the application of the card. Look into both the positive and negative applications of the energy and see which you are manifesting in your life. If there is something you need to work on or change, you now have the chance to do so, as it has been brought to your attention. To be able to succeed in life you need to manifest the positive application of the energy.

If you do not have a particular question, then just pull out a card and Ódinn (the Creator) will give you advice. His expanded awareness knows what you need to examine, and you will be surprised at the insight Ódinn has and the great guidance he gives you for your situation.

THE GUIDANCE OF THOR

Thor was the strongest of all Gods and men, the untamed warrior, who in spite of his unruly manner was the protector of the Gods. He was the red-bearded guardian who rode the heavens in his chariot, pulled by his goats *Tanngnjóstur* and *Tanngrisnir,* with his hammer *Mjölnir* in his hand, always ready for any battle.

The guidance of Thor appears through his strategic skills and ability to find resolutions, as one of his main characteristics was always to find a way out, no matter how cornered he was. He charged fearlessly whatever the assignment was, and usually came out as conqueror. His guidance will give you the strength to assess any situation and continue fearlessly, ready for the next round in life.

You can seek Thor's guidance when you need information on the course of your life in the near future, on your work situation, or a solution to a situation in which you can see no way out. The spread is symbolized by Thor's hammer, Mjölnir.

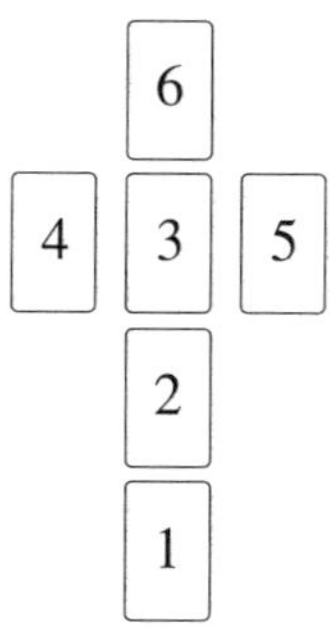

1) This card represents your past, the situation you have just worked your way through, or the dragon you have recently conquered. See what the experience you have just passed through has taught you. Each experience that comes your way is a lesson and you learn both from your failures and successes. So if you failed the first time around, it does not mean you cannot try again. Learning by experience enables you to avoid the mistakes you made last time and gives you an opportunity to do better next time. By doing so, you are always doing your very best.

2) This card represents a new choice that is now available to you. The card shows you what you can do to change the course of your life. Changes usually demand a great effort and sometimes appear to be obstacles in our lives when they first appear. But be on the lookout for new opportunities. Every obstacle that you overcome helps you to take the next step on your path of spiritual growth and provides you with new opportunities in life.

3) This is the center of the spread. It represents you, and shows you the energy you are now in charge of and ways in which you can manifest that energy and use it in your own life. If you have learned from the experience that the first card gave you, this card shows you what energy you possess to apply to the opportunity offered by the second card.

4) This card represents the energy that is working with you in the upcoming changes. However, the energy only works with you if you are able to express the positive aspect of it. If you are still expressing the negative aspect, it will act as a hindrance.

5) This card represents the energy that works against your getting the results you seek. Do not look upon the energy as an enemy, rather as something in your life that

appears as an obstacle which you must learn to overcome. Go Viking and devise a scheme that enables you to master this energy and turn it to your favor, so that you are able to express it positively and use it as an aid in reaching your goals.

6) This card represents the future into which you are heading. This part of the hammer Mjölnir is furthest away from you. Yet it is not so far away that you do not see it. The card shows you what your future can be like if you put an effort into getting there. Read through the positive and negative applications of the card's energy. Take some time and make a list of your future goals. Where do you intend to go Viking with the energy that is now at your disposal? Set yourself a course. The Vikings had sundials to keep their ships on course. A list that covers your future goals works like a sundial and guides you into your future.

THE GUIDANCE OF FREYJA

Freyja, the Goddess of fertility, came from the family of *Vanir* and was the daughter of *Njördur* and the sister of *Freyr.* People worshipped Freyja and Freyr when they wanted fertility (in any form) and beauty in their lives. People called upon Freyja's powers when they wanted beauty and bloom in their love affairs, as she was considered to be the most beautiful of women. She lived in the heavenly realms of *Fólkvangur* ('place of the people') in a palace named *Sessrúmnir* ('room for many seated'), and her rooms were both big and beautiful. Freyja traveled in a chariot pulled by two cats, and when she rode to the battlefields, she claimed half of the *valur* (the slain ones) from Ódinn.

It is best to seek Freyja's guidance when a new time of fertility is beginning in your life. Fertility can be associated with a new task you are taking on, a new love affair or friendship. While reading the spread, examine whether the question relates to something that is at the sowing stage, or whether the matter concerned is already into its growth period.

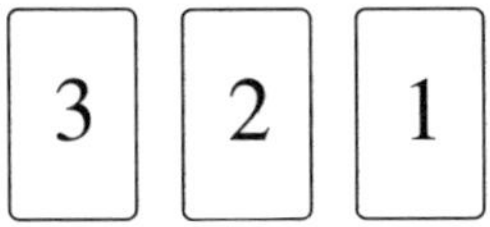

1) This card represents the soil that you sow in. The crop or outcome can never be better than the soil, because it receives its nourishment through the roots in the soil. Take a close look at the soil into which you are sowing your new project.

2) This card represents the growing stage of your project and shows you the possibilities for your project's future growth and development. Your project will only flourish if it enjoys sunshine and fresh air, and is sheltered from the wind. Examine where you need to support and nourish your new project, or whether you need to give it better shelter.

3) This card represents the harvest or outcome of the project and shows you what the final results are likely to be. The one who sows his seeds with care and nourishes everything in his life will reap abundantly. If your project is still at the sowing stage, you can check on what it is you need to do to reap the greatest rewards. However, if the project is something you are working on with another individual, please keep in mind that you both have a free will; if you are not in agreement as to what to do, this can change the outcome now shown as likely by the cards. The spread

indicates a likely picture of the future based on the present situation or energy involved.

THE GUIDANCE OF FORSETI

Forseti was the son of *Baldur,* the handsome and good God, and his wife *Nanna*. Forseti lived in *Ásgardur* (home or garden of the heathen Gods) in a beautiful palace named *Glitnir,* which had a silver roof and golden columns. Forseti's role was to settle any conflict that arose between men or Gods. He was considered to be an excellent arbitrator, and all those who came to him with their conflicts left him reconciled.

The guidance of Forseti allows you to settle any controversy you may feel inside yourself or that may arise between you and others. Forseti offers you a solution to your conflicts through a spread of three cards.

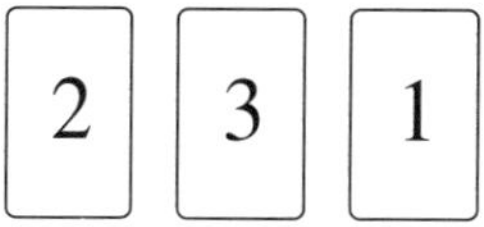

1) This card represents your own partiality. It shows you the angle from which you view the conflict. Is your side of the matter represented by the positive application of the card? Or do you proclaim the negative application as your side of the matter? Look into both the positive and negative applications, and notice how looking at the matter in a broader perspective may lead you to another viewpoint.

2) This card represents your opponent's side. He views the conflict from this point, and according to the way he sees things, this is the right way. Does his view proclaim the positive or the negative application of the card? Is he right

or wrong? Is it possible that if you try to put yourself in his shoes, you gain a better understanding of how he feels about the conflict?

3) This card represents the solution and settlement of the conflict, an impartial solution that respects the views of both parties concerned. It offers you a new viewpoint that can help you solve your conflict. Take note of the guidance of Forseti, because he was the best arbitrator in all conflicts.

THE GUIDANCE OF THE VÖLVA

Through the ages, almost every civilization has had someone who held the status of an oracle, predicted events and foretold the future. When the Vikings wanted information about their future prospects they sought out a *seidmann* or *seidkona* (shaman or shamaness). Shamanesses were sometimes called *völva.* The name can relate to the fact that some of them used *völubein* (knuckle bones) in their shamanic practices. My belief is that most of the shamanesses were also midwives and the name *Völva* can thus be derived from *vulva,* a Latin name for the female genitals. Although the midwives in Iceland stopped foretelling the future a long time ago, most of them kept on being medicine women even until this century, using herbs and plants for healing.

The Völva guides you when you need information on how to develop your intuition and the feminine aspect of your being. Both men and women have a feminine and a masculine aspect. Through your feminine aspect, you develop your sensitivity and intuition. When you seek out the guidance of the Völva, you can expect changes. Therefore the spread represents the five-pointed star, the symbol of the seeker.

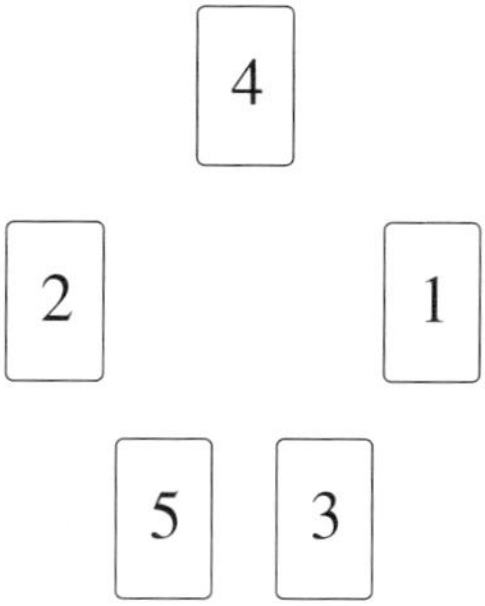

1) This card represents the wisdom you have acquired. This is where you find yourself now, on the threshold of your future. This card gives you information both on what you have already learned (if you are proclaiming the positive application of the energy), and that which you have still to work your way through (the negative application of the energy).

2) This card represents emotional issues from your past that you must resolve before you can continue on your path to spiritual growth. The past sometimes keeps a firm hold on many Spiritual Vikings and prevents them from launching their vessels. Take a close look at which anchor lines must be severed so that you can continue on your journey. Most of the time you are anchored to some inner dragon that you have not dared to face.

3) This card represents the core of truth you must now face. Although you as a human being are seeking greater spiritual growth, you live on Earth. Therefore your growth will be greatest when you balance your spiritual and material lives. To whom do you need to be true? Is it not at all times to yourself? Very often you choose to avoid being true to yourself, while feeling that your loyalty is due others. Now you are forced to face being true to yourself. When you

become true to yourself, you become a Spiritual Viking of great integrity, which reflects upon everything you do.

4) This card teaches you about justice. Are you being just to yourself, as you pass one judgment after the other? Or are you being just to others, whom you relentlessly judge, not seeing that what they are showing you through their behavior is what you dislike most about yourself? Other people are a mirror provided for you to look into. Do you need to take a closer look at some matter of justice, which you have up until now wanted to ignore and even at times thought you could avoid facing altogether? The guidance that this card gives you requires some time alone and a reevaluation of your life and immediate surroundings. If you do that, you will learn to show yourself more tenderness.

5) This card represents your spiritual future. It indicates where your spiritual strength will be in the near future. This is the course you will take as you go Viking, but as you grow and reach new stages of maturity, this place becomes a starting point, because growth is a never-ending cycle.

CARD 1

THE HELMET

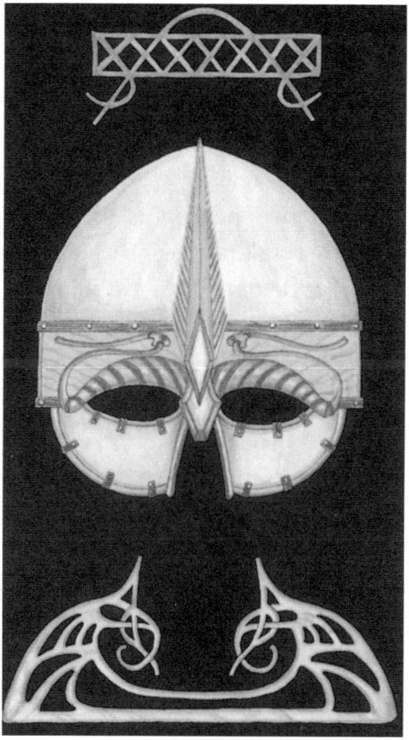

VICTORY

1
THE HELMET - VICTORY

The Vikings used their helmets during battle to protect their heads, a part of the body many considered the most important. The helmets varied in size and shape, depending on what materials were available. Most of the helmets that have been retrieved since the time of the Vikings are simple iron helmets, with or without a nose guard, but a few are impressively adorned. Some of these adorned helmets are considered to have originated in southern parts of the world, whether they were obtained through friendly trade or plundered in warfare. Helmets with horns have not been uncovered, and must therefore be considered to stem from the imagination of later artists who have persistently drawn the Vikings wearing horned helmets. The helmet was part of the military consciousness of the Viking, always worn when heading into battle and only removed at the end of it.

THE POSITIVE APPLICATION:

The Helmet represents Victory for the Spiritual Viking, who wants to conquer all obstacles in his life. If the Helmet has entered your spread today, it is an indication of Victory in some form. Is there a conflict in your immediate surroundings, within yourself or with someone else? If so, you must remember that first-rate preparation leads to Victory. If you are already in the middle of the skirmish, it is important for you to remember that the Helmet will do you little good unless you also use your strategy and cunning. Whether your Victory today is on a small or grand scale, you need to see yourself as being Victorious in life. Your battles are always with your own personality, which wants to keep your Higher Self out of your everyday life. You need to connect with the spiritual being that is you. Victory is usually followed by success, which can be either on the spiritual or material level of your life, or on both. However, as a Spiritual Viking you must take care not to become arrogant simply because you are triumphant.

THE NEGATIVE APPLICATION:

You have already charged into the battle, only to realize that you have forgotten to put on your Helmet. Your impatience barred you from making a strategic plan, and as you have rushed aimlessly into the battle you cannot expect Victory this time around. You might possibly attain Victory if you were to react quickly and change your tactics. By doing so, you might be able to strike the enemy with an unexpected blow; but sometimes the enemy is yourself, as you are fighting something within. If changing tactics is impossible, then you may expect to lose this round in life. But what is one defeat? Is it not an encouragement to the Spiritual Viking to get up again and charge into a new battle, only this time to win?

CARD 2

THE SPEAR

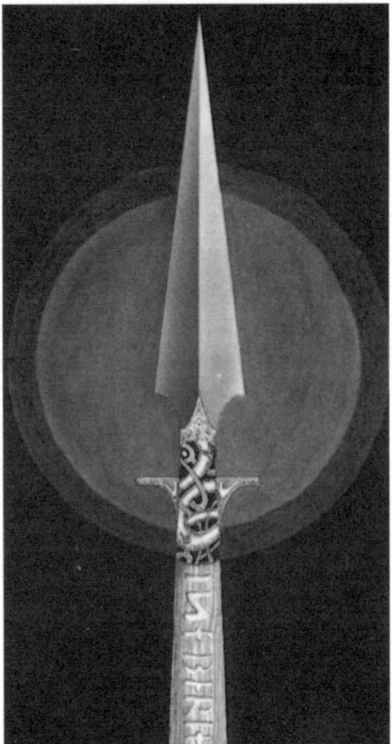

PURPOSE/GOAL

2

THE SPEAR - PURPOSE/GOAL

The spear was one of the main weapons of the Vikings. The life of the Viking relied on accuracy in throwing the spear at its target. The spear was a heavy weapon and demanded skillfulness in handling. Some Vikings were renowned for their skill with the spear, but to become good at using it, they had to build up their physical strength and practice relentlessly. As a stimulant and a challenge to each other, the Vikings competed in different warfare and athletic skills during their gatherings. Many of their competitions were centered around their abilities as warriors, as their lives were based to a great extent on warfare and survival. Ódinn, the supreme God, always traveled with his spear *Gungni,* which he had made his own by carving runes on it. It is therefore likely that each Viking personalized his spear by carving a rune on it.

THE POSITIVE APPLICATION:

The Spear represents your Purpose and Goals in life. It requires self-discipline to set yourself a Goal, and it requires endurance to reach it. If the Spear has appeared in your spread today, it is here to remind you that you need to set Goals for yourself. Are you Purposefully heading somewhere in your life or on your spiritual path, or have you no idea where you are going? If you have a Goal in your life, do you lack the endurance to reach it? This card is here to remind you that every time you throw your Spear, it requires a direct aim so that the Goal can be reached. You may be right on course, but the final spurt requires discipline. Follow each throw of the Spear, and you will be able to reach the Goals at which you aim in a Purposeful way.

The Negative Application:

Your life seems to be void of Goals, and you have nothing to aim at as you throw your Spear. Therefore, as you try to throw the Spear, it lacks all drive and falls down close beside you. You are not successful in life because most of the time there is no Purpose or enthusiasm in what you are doing. Without a Purpose, your life becomes unstable and you move from one thing to another. At times you may feel you know where you want to go or what you want to do, but your Goals seem to be miles away and you keep on telling yourself you cannot reach them. You need to focus on discipline and decisiveness for your life to become Purposeful. That enables you to set your own Goals and to reach them.

CARD 3

HUGINN AND MUNINN

MESSAGES

3

HUGINN AND MUNINN - MESSAGES

Huginn and Muninn were the ravens of Ódinn, and they were symbolic of his logical mind and intuition. Every morning they flew out over the world and returned at night, placing themselves on the shoulders of Ódinn and telling him what they had seen. They brought him tidings of what had already happened in the world or was about to take place. Their black color reminds us of the unknown areas within ourselves, those areas we are sometimes reluctant to explore out of fear for what we might discover.

The Vikings considered the raven a wise bird, and took ravens along on journeys to distant places. It is common knowledge that when Iceland was settled the Vikings had ravens on board their ships, and when they thought they were close to the country, they set the ravens free. The Vikings used them as a criterion: if they returned to the ship, land was still far ahead; but if they did not, it was close by.

THE POSITIVE APPLICATION:

Huginn represents your logical mind, and Muninn represents your intuition. You receive Messages through both of them. If Huginn and Muninn have flown into your spread today, they are here to bring you Messages. Their Messages can take on many forms and touch upon various aspects of your life. It is even possible that you do not clearly understand the Messages they are trying to relay to you right away, and that some time may pass before you identify them. As you look for the Messages, use your senses, listen, open your heart and logical mind, and trust your intuition. Dreams and premonitions can also be ways in which the Messages are reaching you. A subtle change in your everyday life carries a Message. Listen to your body, which may need a better diet or some rest. To gain your attention and care, the body may be sending you Messages through discomfort or fatigue. Messages that can help or guide you may also be relayed through people around you, or through workshops or books. However the Messages reach you, whether through things or through the people in your life, they are always aimed at you. Difficulties in a relationship with someone indicate that there is something you need to look at in your own behavior, not that there is something the other person needs to deal with (they may, but then it is their issue). Open up your senses and you will discover that identifying the Messages that Huginn and Muninn bring you expands your spiritual growth and helps you enjoy a better life as a Spiritual Viking.

The Negative Application:

You do not notice that Huginn and Muninn are circling around you, and therefore you are unable to acknowledge their Messages. Your senses are completely blocked and you are unable to receive any guidance. Their attempt to reach you can be compared to the telephone ringing in your home and you not picking it up to answer. That is how the ravens perceive your disconnection. You do not grasp their Messages, although your body may be experiencing discomfort, you are unhappy with life, your relationships are not working, or you are discontented at work. You focus outwards and blame others for your circumstances, unable to see that the Messages are aimed at you. Sometimes your immediate environment is like a mirror, and the reflection it sends back is that of you. Look in the mirror and see whether you can perceive the Messages Huginn and Muninn are trying to relay to you through others.

CARD 4

THE SOLSTICE CAIRN

LIGHT OF LIFE

4

THE SOLSTICE CAIRN - LIGHT OF LIFE

In many places throughout Iceland, fully-stacked and still-intact stone cairns, or ruins of stone cairns, can be found. These cairns do not correlate to the old beaten tracks or walking trails of the country, although these were marked with small stone cairns. These cairns were stacked for a purpose other than guiding the traveler on land. They represented man's connection with the source of the Light of Life, the Sun. The Solstice Cairns are stacked in places where the Sun forms a lay-line southwest/northeast through the country at Summer and Winter Solstice. The Sun played a very important part in the life of the Vikings. They understood that it was the force that kindled all life, and that without the Sun there would be nothing. The Sun provided them with more than warmth and light for their fields. When sailing, the Vikings used sundials. They owned charts that indicated the altitude of the Sun as it rose and set, and by using these charts and the sundials they could set their course when sailing the seas. When the settlers decided to assemble an *Althing* (Council of All) in Iceland, it was done at Summer Solstice (and continued to be held at that time). *Thingvellir* (translates as 'Plains of the Council') was selected as the site of the Althing because of its geological bearings and connection to the lay-lines of the country.

The Positive Application:

The Solstice Cairn represents the Light of Life. The Sun is only the outer expression of the Spiritual Light that dwells behind it. If the Solstice Cairn, with its bright beams of Light, is present in your spread today, it is here to remind you that the Light of Life shines brightly on you, or that soon it will clear the dark times you may have experienced. In a way similar to the course of the Sun here in the northern part of the world, where summers have twenty-four hours of daylight, and where there are short winter days when the Sun barely crawls up over the horizon before it disappears again, we all experience times of Light and darkness in our lives. Therefore, it is of greatest importance for you to realize that the Sun always shines, even when you can't see it. By making an effort to always see the positive aspect of things, you as a Spiritual Viking are bringing more Light into your life. A positive attitude ensures that you are always immersed in the Light of Life, whatever the weather.

The Negative Application:

Although the Solstice Cairn is present in your spread today, you cannot visualize any Light in your own existence. You have surrendered to the darkness and the negative forces. Your own darkness can become so dense that you cannot see the Light of Life, even when the Sun is shining directly on you. Everyone around you is aware of the Light, but that is of little help if you do not see it yourself. Your understanding of the Light of Life must come from within. If you want to become a Spiritual Viking, you must draw back the dark curtains in your own mind so that the Light can reach you. Doing so does not have to be a great effort. But you must be willing to change and ready to open your mind and heart to receive the Light of Life. The only incentive you need is a positive way of thinking.

CARD 5

THE HEARTH

CARE

5

THE HEARTH - CARE

The Vikings who settled in Iceland usually brought wood for their first houses from Norway, Ireland or England, and built longhouses as dwellings. Later their architecture changed, as they adapted themselves to the weather and environmental conditions in Iceland and to the building material available in the country. The longhouses were furnished with a hearth along the middle of the floor to keep everyone warm. They were therefore true *eldhús* (a house of fire). The fire represents the Sun, and the word 'eldhús' has sometimes been interpreted as 'the house of the Sun.' The hearth definitely kept the household warm, but it was also used for cooking. By the hearth, the housewife prepared the nourishment for her household and her guests. Preparation of the food allowed the housewife to show the care she had for everyone, and most housewives strived to make sure that there was no shortage of food at their hearth.

THE POSITIVE APPLICATION:

The Hearth represents Care, both self-Care and Care for others. If the Hearth warms up your spread today, it is here to teach you about Caring. To be able to Care for and nourish others, you must first learn how to Care for yourself. You must learn to nourish your body, your mind and your spirit before you can take Care of others. The Hearth encourages you to make available the Care and nourishment you now need. If you have already learned to Care for yourself, then the Hearth encourages you to Care for those around you and shoulder the responsibilities you have agreed to take on for your family and friends. Caring is a wonderful force that creates healing and nourishment through touch, words or behavior. When you Care for others, the feeling of Care resonates back to you, and you receive Care from them.

The Negative Application:

Although the Hearth is in your spread today, you neither notice nor value the Care of others, mainly because you have not learned to Care for yourself. You deny your own needs and pretend to be able to bypass them forever. You make believe you are Caring for everyone around you, but that Caring has long since turned into its opposite, materializing as overprotection and a need to control everything around you. Caring does not entitle you to control the life of other people. It only allows you to show them the same tenderness and tolerance you need to be showing yourself. You need to revalue your understanding of the word 'Care,' let go of your judgmental attitude and show yourself some tenderness. Everything in your life begins with yourself; having learned to Care for yourself, you can then Care for others.

CARD 6

THE LIBELOUS POLE

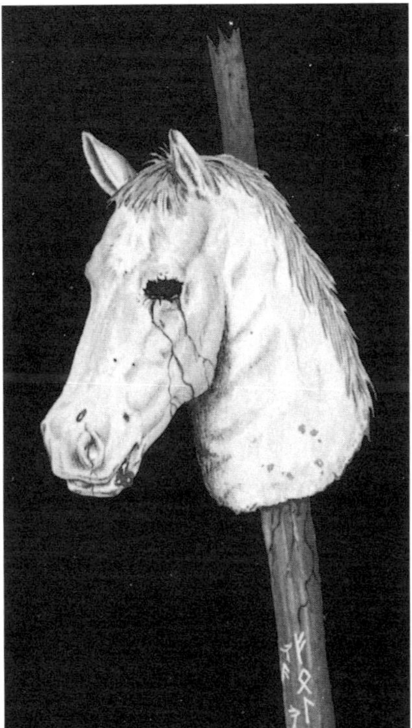

COMMUNICATION

6

THE LIBELOUS POLE - COMMUNICATION

The Vikings were in the custom of erecting a libelous pole in disdain of those with whom they had malicious disputes. At the top of the libelous pole, they usually put the head of a dead horse and had it face the direction of the person toward whom the libel was aimed. Sometimes the roots of a libel could be traced back to misinterpretation of something a person had said or done, or to a courier who had misinterpreted the message he was to deliver.

Having a libelous pole aimed at you was a great disgrace and the erection of one was sometimes the spark that ignited more fury in a dispute. That fury sometimes led to the slaying of men. In the social structure of the Vikings, revenge for all offenses was considered a normal part of life, and the Vikings did not fear death. However, constant revenge between families sometimes went to extremes, and arbitrators had to intercede between the conflicting parties in order to make a truce by offering monetary or other compensations to settle the dispute and end the killings.

THE POSITIVE APPLICATION:

The Libelous Pole represents Communication in your life. If the Libelous Pole has been erected in your spread today, it is here to remind you that all talk requires discretion and caution. Words spoken without compassion cannot be retrieved, therefore one should always be discreet. Take care that your idle talk about others has a positive undertone and supports reconstruction rather than demolition of reputation. There may be times when you are unaware of how sharp your tongue is.

Not all talk is idle talk, so you need to be clear in your Communication with people around you, telling them how you feel, what you think and what you would like to do. Most problems arise when people are not clear in their Communication with each other. Lack of clear Communication often creates a misunderstanding that can lead to the raising of Libelous Poles, something that might easily be avoided by speaking one's mind clearly.

The Libelous Pole can also be pointing out to you that you are the subject of other people's idle talk. Someone's praise is the positive form of idle talk, and it is important to be able to receive that with gratitude in mind.

The Negative Application:

The Libelous Pole is a reminder that you spend too much time talking idly about what you are going to do, but never get around to doing. Your talk also revolves a lot around others, and sometimes that talk has a negative undertone. Stop speculating about other people's lives and get your own together. If everything in your life revolves around idle talk, that is an indication that you do not Communicate clearly with yourself and others. Try to improve your own Communication skills. No glory is associated with negative idle talk about others; it only indicates a touch of envy.

The Libelous Pole can also be indicating that someone's idle talk about you is spiteful and negative. You need to pay attention to those around you and try to discover the nature of their idle talk. Keep in mind that the nature of idle talk is a reflection of how the speaker feels about himself, and negative idle talk most of the time stems from his own feelings of inferiority. Such feelings deserve understanding rather than revenge or the erection of a Libelous Pole.

CARD 7

THE COUNCIL

DECISION

7
THE COUNCIL - DECISION

Iceland's parliamentary council was formally assembled in the year 930 at Thingvellir and is considered by many to be the oldest parliamentary or council rule known in the western world. Iceland was subdivided into 36 *godord* (sections of land ruled by the *godi,* who was priest-chieftain), and each of the 36 priest-chieftains embodied the idea of the four elements, each holding 1/36 of the sacred circle – the crown of state. In every godord there was a place where smaller councils were held, but a joint council was held at Thingvellir once a year and called *Althing* (Council of All). To Althing rode all the priest-chieftains from each godord, with their escort. The site of Althing was important, and its location at Thingvellir was demarcated (*markat* in Old Icelandic), fixed and measured. The Althing also had *vébönd,* ropes which marked certain places where weapons were not to be carried and peace was to be maintained. At the council the 36 godar jointly settled all matters that had not been resolved in their own godord.

At this joint summer council at Thingvellir, which met at Summer Solstice and lasted for two weeks, the time was not only used for settling disputes, but also for showing oneself and seeing others, and for arranging marriages and trade matters. The council was also the site of competitions and various games, where people had a chance to show off their skills. Emissaries from foreign heads of state also visited the

Althing when they had an errand with the Icelandic nation. *Lögrétta* was the legislative court of Althing, but *Lögberg* (law rock) was the place where speeches were delivered and the law recited. The Althing was formally opened by the *allsherjargodi* (chief godi of the country), the one that ruled the godord of *Ingólfur Arnarson* (believed to be the first settler in Iceland), but the *lögsögumadur* (law-sayer who knew the law) ruled the council.

THE POSITIVE APPLICATION:

The Council represents Decisions made in your life, both by yourself and by others. If the Council is meeting in your spread today, it indicates that you as a Spiritual Viking need to make a Decision. When you make a Decision, it is often good to seek the opinion of others and get help with evaluating the circumstances. It is important to be aware of every angle of each matter, and not to exclude other people's viewpoints, especially if your Decision will affect them. When you have discussed your situation with friends, a Decision needs to be made. That Decision can only be made by you, as you alone are responsible for your own life. You are truly the law-sayer in your life, because the final Decision in all matters rests with you. Bear in mind that whatever Decision you make, it is always the correct one for this moment; if circumstances change, you can always make a new Decision. The question is never about what is right or wrong, only about making a Decision and doing what you need to do. If your Decision does not bring about the results you expected, you need to re-examine it. The Council may also indicate that people around you are making Decisions they are not allowing you to be part of. Be aware in that kind of situation.

The Negative Application:

You spend all your time in Council, constantly seeking advice from others on what to do in your situation. But even when you seem to have reached the appropriate solution, you lack the courage to follow through on it. Too many viewpoints in a simple matter create confusion. Going from one person to another seeking advice leads to a situation where you are tossed around in an overflow of opinions, only becoming more undecided all the time. You choose to hide behind excuses about not being able to Decide, but at the same time you experience a complete stagnation in matters that demand your Decision. Stagnation is a form of death. Decisions help you move forward on the eternal spiral of life, and therefore they must be made.

CARD 8

PLACE OF POWER

SACRED PLACE/INNER PEACE

8

PLACE OF POWER - SACRED PLACE/INNER PEACE

Iceland is a country bountiful with powerful Earth/Nature energy, and there are many very powerful energy spots in different areas of the island. For this card I have chosen a picture of the mountain *Helgafell* at *Thorsnes,* south of *Stykkishólmur.* Since the early settlement days of the Vikings, Helgafell has been considered a sacred and magnetic place of power. Helgafell is not a high mountain, but climbing it today one follows certain rules. You start your journey at a fixed point and walk up to the top of the mountain without looking back or uttering a word. That tradition is old, and helps you keep a focus on what you will pray for at the top of the mountain. When you reach the top (there is a type of stone cairn or shelter there) you face northeast, where the Sun comes up at Summer Solstice, and call upon the God you want to communicate with. It is said that if you follow these rules, you will be granted three wishes.

Helgafell was used during pagan times for *útisetur,* or vision questing, both by those who resided there and by others. The Vikings believed nature spirits and beings from other dimensions resided in places in nature such as mountains, and they used those with the greatest source of energy as sacred places for communicating with the Creator. Helgafell was one such place, considered to be the most sacred of all. In fact, the name *Helgafell* means 'the holy mountain.' Since the early days of settlement in Iceland, many individuals known from the Sagas lived at Helgafell, but the most famous ones are probably *Snorri godi* (chieftain) *Thorgrímsson* and *Gudrún Ósvífursdóttir*, known from the *Laxdæla Saga*, who prior to living at Helgafell lived at *Sælingsdal*. Gudrún and Snorri exchanged lands, and Gudrún then moved to Helgafell where she is buried.

THE POSITIVE APPLICATION:

The Place of Power represents your own Sacred Place. Your Sacred Place is any site you can turn to in nature, or a refuge at home where you can enjoy quiet moments, calm your mind and meditate, or practice shamanism. Communicating with nature releases negative energy from the body and heals the body. The same applies to a quiet moment indoors, although being in the presence of nature is more powerful. If the Place of Power has situated itself in your spread today, it is implying that you have to honor your need for solitude and Inner Peace. A moment spent in meditation and quiet recharges your physical and mental energy fields. If your Sacred Place is outdoors, it gives nature a chance to nourish you.

Where is your favorite place in nature? Select that spot as your Place of Power and visit it regularly, or find a quiet moment at home and journey through the inner worlds to that place. You can create an even stronger bond with your Sacred Place in nature by taking a crystal or a stone from that Place of Power, and hold it in your hands as you journey. It is very important to learn to calm the mind and take charge of it. The mind often wants to run in any direction like a wild animal, but when we learn to manage it, we are able to utilize it as a tool in our spiritual growth and development. Taming and quieting the mind strengthens us as Spiritual Vikings.

The Negative Application:

You absolutely renounce your need for Inner Peace and communication with nature, and do not believe that you need a Place of Power. You are unaware of the unlimited source of energy that nature provides you with, and you are unconscious of the fact that it is yours to tap into. Any notion about managing your mind through meditation is far-removed from you, yet you find it hard to accept how untamed your mind is. If you want to be in charge of your own life, you need to explore the inner realms of your being; and to be able to journey through these spaces, stillness needs to reign. Therefore, it is necessary to seek out your own Sacred Place, and through the Inner Peace with which that place provides you, to enjoy more fullness in your life.

CARD 9

THE RUNE

MYSTERY

9

THE RUNE - MYSTERY

The very discovery of the Runes can be traced back to Ódinn. He fasted for nine days and nine nights, hanging upside down on the sacred tree Yggdrasill at the center of the world, bleeding from a self-inflicted wound from his spear. By sacrificing himself, he sought the mysterious truth of all life, a symbol of more wisdom than he already possessed. On the ninth day, when he hadn't discovered any truth, his hands reached in desperation into *Mímisbrunnur,* the well of abundant wisdom that is under one of the three roots of Yggdrasill. When his hands came out of the ice-cold water again, they were clutching the sacred Runes. By holding them, he acquired the magic and power he had sought. After the fasting, he claimed his own spear by carving a Rune on it. He also carved the Runes onto other things, claimed them and thus had power over everything in the world. The word 'Rune' means mystery, and those that could unravel the mysteries were oracles. In spite of Ódinn's shamanic and transformative powers, he yearned to know more; in doing so, he discovered that what he sought most had always been right in front of him. He just hadn't seen it. The same often applies to the Spiritual Viking.

The Positive Application:

The Rune represents the Mystery of life, and one of the greatest Mysteries lies in connecting with the Divine power within yourself, a power you aren't always aware of as it is so close to you. If the Rune has carved its way into your spread today, it is an indication of Mysteries that will soon be revealed to you. Life offers you endless Mysteries. The only thing you need to do is to fathom them and learn to appreciate them. Mystery resides in the beauty of the Sun and the Moon, in the ever-changing cloud formations, in the intense power of the Northern Lights (*aurora borealis*) or in detecting the hidden messages of the wind. Mysteries are all around you, but you have lost touch with nature, and your ability to grasp the Mysteries has vanished. Your Mysteries manifest themselves through your ability to laugh and put Love and Light into everything you do. Mysteries are also revealed through your adaptability in your relationships with people, places, and possessions, and in your expanded awareness of who you are.

The Negative Application:

You are unable to see the Mysteries of life that the Rune tries to unveil for you, even when they are right in front of your eyes. Like Ódinn in the tree Yggdrasill, you need to suffer a great deal before you can appreciate the little things in your life, or see that it is you who holds the answers to the solutions you are seeking. Only you can put an end to that suffering, by lifting the veil from your eyes and seeing the Mysteries within and all around you. Things are never as complicated as they seem to be; you only make them so.

CARD 10

THE GOD

PRAYER/TRUST

10
THE GOD - PRAYER/TRUST

There were many *god* in the pagan hierarchy, but the most commonly worshipped Gods seem to have been Thor, Ódinn and Freyr. Thor was closest to the Vikings. He was the God of the common man and thus worshipped by most people. Ódinn was the God of chieftains, poets and shamans, and he was worshipped for victory in battles and when men went Viking. He was also worshipped by poets who sought poetic inspiration. In *Snorra-Edda* it is written that Freyr "rules the rain and the brightness of the Sun and therefore the fruit of the Earth," so he was worshipped as the God of fertility, water and light. Archaeological findings in Iceland have mostly revealed symbols of Thor and Freyr. Although the image that the Vikings had of Ódinn was colorful, only a few symbols of him have been discovered.

The Vikings placed the symbols of their Gods in their *hof* or temples, which I believe were mostly outdoors. In the pagan belief, the sacred sites were called *vé,* places one only entered with awe and respect. The statues of the Gods represented beings from higher dimensions who possessed more power than human beings. When people worshipped the *god*, they were seeking guidance and help from the Higher Power that each of the Gods represented.

THE POSITIVE APPLICATION:

The God represents Prayer and Trust. If the God has

claimed your spread with its presence today, it is here to remind you that you need to connect with the Divine power. You need to reinstate your Trust in the Creator and learn to communicate with the Divine Father/Mother by praying. Through Trust and Prayer you can turn the Divine spark that was given to you at birth into a loving Light which radiates through all your deeds, and you appear as a reflection of the Divine power here on Earth. Through Prayer you also learn to empower yourself, and gain more confidence and the ability to manage your own life. Prayer enables you to seek help not only from the Creator, but also from your spiritual guides and other Light Beings. In nature you can call upon the powers of the devas and fairies to help you cultivate and heal the Earth. Trust teaches you to rely on the guidance you receive from the higher dimensions, although you do not see these Beings with your outer vision, but only sense them through your inner vision.

THE NEGATIVE APPLICATION:

The God is a reminder that there is little Trust in your life. You find it difficult to believe in a Divine existence, but through your disbelief you also renounce the Divine aspect of yourself. Your lack of Trust is also reflected in your lack of confidence. You proclaim that no Creator exists, as he has never helped you, but you have never Prayed and asked for help. As soon as you Pray and ask for help, you open up a channel of energy for help to reach you. Renouncing Trust isolates you and makes you even more unsure of who you are. You need to get rid of this renunciation and accept that through the Divine spark within you, you are able to connect with the Creator or any of his positive Light-giving forces through Prayer, and thus invite strength and harmony into your life.

CARD 11

THE TOTEM POLES

SPIRITUAL GUIDANCE

11

THE TOTEM POLES - SPIRITUAL GUIDANCE

The Totem Poles were sacred symbols of the Vikings. They were either placed on both sides of the seat of honor (male's seat) in the homes of the Vikings or at their sacred places of worship (*vé*). Whenever the Vikings moved their dwellings, the Totem Poles were taken along, as was the case when they moved to Iceland. To the owner, the Totem Poles were a symbolic link between the physical and spiritual dimension (Heaven and Earth) and were as such a route for spiritual guidance. When the Vikings were close enough to Iceland to sight land, they threw their Totem Poles overboard and claimed land where the Poles drifted ashore. Their belief was that the Gods had chosen a place for them that was theirs whether it was at a good or a bad location. Sometimes it took quite a while to locate the Totem Poles. But the Vikings persevered, firmly believing the Gods would lead them to their destined land which was theirs alone to settle.

THE POSITIVE APPLICATION:

The Totem Poles represent Spiritual Guidance in your life. If the Totem Poles have drifted into your spread today, they are telling you to rely on Guidance and support from your Higher Power in life. Fearlessly cast your Totem Poles overboard and trust that they will drift ashore at the right location. Show courage and patience, and trust that the Spiritual Guidance and support you receive will lead you to where your life's work will be of the greatest service, both to you and to others around you. The Vikings sometimes had to search through more than one summer for their Totem Poles, but never lost faith in Spiritual Guidance. Sometimes you need to stay in the same place for a while and rest before you continue your search. Resting can apply to you now, but before too long you will find your own Totem Poles, which will then lead you to new opportunities in life.

THE NEGATIVE APPLICATION:

Your impatience gets in the way and you feel you do not have enough time to find your own Totem Poles. By feeling that way, you lose sight of the Spiritual Guidance and Support you are getting. You either settle for not finding your Totem Poles (your own destiny) at all, or you try taking over ones that belong to others. Every individual has chosen a certain path in life and experiences he intends to gain. You cannot exchange your experience in life for someone else's, although at times theirs may seem more appealing. You need to accept the role you have in life as yours. Only then can you start working on the changes you want to make. Open your eyes to see where Spiritual Guidance and support is trying to get through to you, and what you need to do in order to receive it. Show patience. Life only passes you by if you do not take the time to live it.

CARD 12

EAST · THE DRAGON

INNER FEAR

12

EAST - THE DRAGON - INNER FEAR

The Vikings believed very strongly that Earth spirits resided in the mountains and hills of Iceland. Some were more powerful than others, and they were the protective guardian spirits of the country. A story of these guardian spirits is told in *Snorri Sturluson's Heimskringla*, one of the most famous Sagas of Iceland. The Vikings had great respect for these guardian spirits, and as an indication of that they passed a law at Althing, stating that if their ships had prows with 'gaping heads' they were to remove them so as not to upset the guardian spirits when approaching the country. Belief in the guardian spirits was not lost, though the heathen Gods and pagan beliefs were outlawed. On the contrary, faith in the spirits lived on; the best proof of that is Iceland's coat of arms, which carries the guardian spirits of the four directions: the Dragon for the east, the Giant for the south, the Bull for the west, and the Eagle for the north. Most of the Vikings first sighted the east or southeast coast of the island as they came from Norway, Scotland, the Hebrides or Ireland, and it is therefore only natural that the Dragon, which is the most frightful of the country's guardian spirits, is the guardian of the east coast. He appeared in *Vopnafjördur.*

THE POSITIVE APPLICATION:

The Dragon represents your Inner Fear. Although the Dragons of the old heroic epics have long since disappeared, you are still unconsciously fighting Dragons that reside within you. They now take on different shapes, like those of self-deprecation, fear, anxiety, greed, jealousy and envy, to name a few. If the Dragon has spouted his fire into your spread today, he is challenging you to wrestle with him. In the old heroic epics, the heroes charged directly at the Dragon to slay it, and that is what you must also do. You have to face your Inner Fears and comprehend their size and magnitude before you can slay them. You need to work toward a positive evaluation of yourself, build up your self-respect, get away from the tyranny of fear, and calm the waves of greed, jealousy and envy. One of the best ways to face the Dragon is to write down what it is that you fear the most. Once you have put the fear on paper, the Dragon won't appear as malicious. Take a look at which Dragon you need to face now and select a positive approach to wrestle with him.

The Negative Application:

You choose continually to run away from the Dragon, instead of wrestling with him. To stay on the run can be very tiring and causes an ever-increasing Inner Fear. The only way to change that situation is to stop running and move from the defensive to the offensive. Thus you challenge yourself to face your own Inner Fears and deal with them accordingly. The negative application of the Dragon can also be that you allow it to take over your life. Your life becomes permeated with some or all of the feelings that reflect through greed, jealousy, fear, anxiety or lack of self-esteem, and emanate from the Dragon. By allowing the Dragon to dominate your life, you stop managing your own personality. Your Higher Self has no way of coming through. The only way out is to seek help and support from others while you build up enough courage to turn around and face the Dragon and deal with it.

CARD 13

SOUTH · THE GIANT

THE INNER CHILD

13

SOUTH - THE GIANT - INNER CHILD

Some of the Vikings that arrived at the east coast of Iceland headed up along the east coast and then along the north coast, while others headed south. We will follow those that went south and thus clockwise around the island. The guardian spirit of the south coast was the Giant. He appeared at *Víkarskeid* on *Reykjanes* and headed eastward along the southern part of Iceland. According to descriptions, the Giant was enormous in size, and traveled with an iron pole in his hand. In spite of his height, he was friendly and created that sense of security which children receive from loving grown-ups. The Giant guards the south coast of the country, where the surf runs high and no harbor can be found anywhere on the main coast, only at the far ends to the east or west. The lack of harbor on the coast didn't hinder the Vikings from going ashore, as their ships were built with a flat keel so that they could go ashore almost anywhere, but the surf may have been an obstacle for them. The Giant needs his height to oversee the flat land he guards, in order to have a good view over the land and the ocean. The ocean represents the depth of our feelings, the hidden feelings from our past that still 'swell under the surface,' and appear from time to time in high and dangerous waves.

THE POSITIVE APPLICATION:

The Giant represents your emotional past and your Inner

Child. If the Giant has walked into your spread today, he is telling you that you need to connect with the Child within and clear blockages from your past. Everything that has at one time or another hurt the Child within you, and that you have hidden in the depths of your soul from the very beginning of your life, must be confronted. Every physical, emotional, mental or spiritual affliction that is not dealt with becomes like a fraction of the soul that is left behind. The soul is not complete if many particles are left behind along your path of life. You need to work on matters from your past and retrieve the lost parts of your soul, so that it can become whole and united again. That unity creates within you a new sense of balance, and allows you to face your present and future with more courage and equilibrium. The Giant guards you while you work your way through the difficulty of your past and is like a big, caring father to your Inner Child. He teaches you fearlessness and fills you with feelings of security and trust toward life.

THE NEGATIVE APPLICATION:

The Giant arouses fear within you, because he rummages through your past and threatens the Child within, who you have so cleverly hidden behind your emotions. The size of the Giant fills you with a sense of your past experiences being larger and more frightening than they really are. Look into the eyes of the Giant and see that they are gentle. Stop running away from your own feelings and put some work into retrieving and uniting the fractions of your soul. Deal with your past experiences, re-connect with the Child within and head fearlessly into the future, filled with the confidence and trust of the Child. The Giant will take you by the hand and lead you through the perils of your past, if you are willing to accept his support.

CARD 14

WEST · THE BULL

ABUNDANCE

14

WEST - THE BULL - ABUNDANCE

The Bull is a big animal that can feed many people. It is very symbolic that this animal of Abundance comes forth as the guardian spirit of the west and appears in *Breidifjördur.* Since the beginning of settlement in Iceland, Breidifjördur has been one of the main food supplying areas of the island. It was filled with fowl and fish, and no one that lived there ever had to suffer from lack or hunger. The Bull, spirit of Abundance, shows us how generously we are provided for on this Earth, that there is plenty to feed and keep everyone, if we are only moderate and learn to share instead of being overcome by greed.

THE POSITIVE APPLICATION:

The Bull represents the Abundance of life. If the Bull has charged into your spread today, it is there to remind you of Abundance. Lack is only a way of thinking, something you fall into when you don't appreciate the Abundance of what you have. Start appreciating everything you already have: your health, home, family, friends and job. Then take a look at how willing you are to receive more into your life, and by which standards you measure Abundance. Abundance is at the threshold of your life, waiting for you to believe it is there and for you to start receiving and allowing it, in whatever form it comes, to become a part of your life. Believe that the universe is Abundant and will supply you with everything you need – but remember at the same time that sometimes your needs can be superfluous. The Bull asks you to look realistically at your needs and appreciate the Abundance of your life from that standpoint.

The Negative Application:

The Bull is to you a symbol of everything you would like to have. However, you are unable to have it, as you have locked yourself away in a world of lack. You wake up every morning only thinking of what you need, not seeing everything you have. Your point of satisfaction is hard to reach as you always demand more. You can be rich or poor, have little or a lot, but if you always think in terms of 'lack' you always need more, no matter how much you get. Therefore, Abundance finds no easy way into your life while you suffer from lack in your mental world. As soon as you stop saying "I need" and start saying "I have," you open up to the Abundance of the Universe.

CARD 15

NORTH · THE EAGLE

OVERVIEW

15

NORTH - THE EAGLE - OVERVIEW

The guardian spirit of the north appeared in *Eyjafjördur.* It was an enormous Eagle, with a wingspan so wide that the tips of the wings reached from one mountain range, across the *fjördur* (bay) over to the other. The Eagle is a majestic bird that soars higher than any other and has often been linked with the Divine energy, for he is said to come closer to the Sun than any other creature. The wingspan of the Eagle grants him great endurance and allows him to float through the skies, while his sharp eyes detect the slightest movement on Earth, so that he is able to see his prey from miles away. The Eagle is the king of all birds, and from the north he has an overview of the whole country and is able to observe everything that happens. The north is also the direction of Ódinn, and the Eagle was one of his power animals. The Eagle is a wise bird that is not easily caught. Other animals rarely dupe him, so he is mostly threatened only by man.

THE POSITIVE APPLICATION:

The Eagle represents the Overview you have of your own life. If the Eagle has flown into your spread today, he is sharing his wisdom with you and helping you to gain an Overview of your life. The Eagle encourages you to be bold enough to fly above the clouds, rely on the support of the winds of the heavens, and thus gain an Overview. Broaden your perspective and learn how to see the greater picture. Put yourself in the place of those around you and sense their feelings and thoughts. Take some time to glide while you evaluate the circumstances, and acquire an Overview before you make your next move. Become aware of where you are situated in the greater picture of life and how your decisions will affect that picture.

The Eagle also encourages you to take on the spiritual flight, and seek ways in which you can truly become a Spiritual Viking and connect with your soul. The Eagle shows you that matter and spirit are inseparable in every realm of the Universe. Both have to work in unison so that the light of your soul and your Divine Spark can illuminate your everyday life. If you are able to connect the two, you become an Eagle every day; a human being in a physical reality, but in direct contact with your Divine Self.

The Negative Application:

The Eagle reminds you that you lack an Overview of your life. Your viewpoint is characterized by narrow-mindedness. You are inclined to see only the minor details and remain stuck there. Solutions are hard to come by and you make life hardest on yourself. This perspective creates pain that affects no one as much as yourself. Another negative application of the Eagle may be that you soar into the heights of the heavens and glide around in a dream state, but forget that your life takes place on Earth. Thus your existence on Earth becomes unsuccessful in many ways, but you excuse yourself by saying that you are so spiritual that you cannot be bothered. Spiritual growth is of little use if you cannot apply it to the material world where you live.

CARD 16

THE VIKING SHIP

EXPLORATION

16

THE VIKING SHIP - EXPLORATION

The Viking ships were extraordinary vessels; built from prime wood, broad, with a shallow draft, and able to carry many men. Either sails or oars were used to sail the ships. During the Viking times, the ships gave the Vikings opportunities to travel far and wide through the territory that we now call Europe, across the seas, and along rivers and canals. The Vikings were great navigators, courageous and filled with a yearning for adventures; a yearning which led them to explore and settle in many areas in the northern part of Europe, in the Faeroe Islands, Iceland, and Greenland; as well as sailing to *Vesturheimur,* that we now know as America; to *Mikligardur* (now Istanbul); and through the territory we have known until recently as the Soviet Union. They did not fear unknown territories or new harbors, as they boldly embarked on the adventures their lives revolved around. Wherever they went they traded, and were introduced to new peoples and customs; if need be, they used their military skills in defense or attack, and plundered if victory was theirs. Their lifestyle reflected the times they lived in, and had to be filled with instant resolutions, courage and vigor.

THE POSITIVE APPLICATION:

The Viking Ship represents the Explorer in you, who wants to head into the uncharted territories of your inner world. If the Viking Ship has sailed into your spread today, it is encouraging you to undertake further Exploration. Moving forward on your path of spiritual growth can only be done step by step. On that path, as on many others, you will often find yourself at a crossroads; at such moments you may need the courage and vigor to select routes which are not traveled by many. The Viking Ship encourages you to jump on board and sail your ship into the inner worlds of your reality, where the actual Exploration takes place today. As you undertake that journey, you will be captain of your vessel and travel through territories which you had not known existed. You will have an opportunity to expand your awareness through such practices as shamanism (or meditation), and these practices will guide you as you explore. Reading books about personal/spiritual growth, participating in workshops, and sharing opinions with others of like mind all lead to an expansion of your awareness. It is up to you to have the courage to choose the path most suited to you, as you continue to follow your heart. As you grow, so does your courage, which allows you to follow through on your growth by changing your lifestyle.

The Negative Application:

The Viking Ship arouses an anxiety within you, because you deny your desire to explore the inner worlds. You feel secure in the comfort of your life today, and you are reluctant to move from that safety. Yearning for adventure was in the blood of the Vikings, but if they had never lifted their anchors, they would never have sailed away to explore unknown territories, nor would they have experienced the wonders their travels brought them. They could have moored in the same fjord all their lives, and the same can be said about your life. If you do not gather up enough courage to face the 'uncharted territory' of the inner worlds, your life will always be at a standstill. Try to find ways to launch your Viking Ship and start the inner Exploration you have renounced up until now.

CARD 17

THE SWEAT LODGE

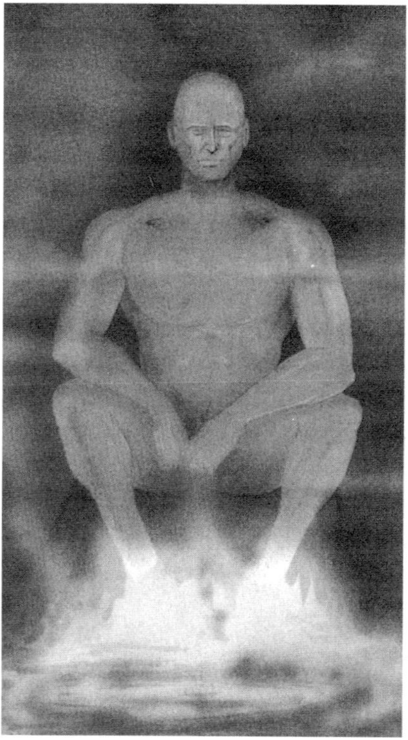

CLEANSING

17

THE SWEAT LODGE - CLEANSING

Most of the time the Vikings only had access to cold water, so they adapted their way of cleansing to those conditions. When they traveled, their sweat lodges were usually made from a framework of twigs covered with a hide; but where they resided for any longer period of time, they built small sweat lodges from available timber. Whichever way the lodge was built, they built a fire outside where they heated stones that were then carried into the lodge, where water was poured over them to create steam in which people cleansed themselves. The clear and cold water in nearby brooks or lakes was then used either for dipping into or splashing onto the body, to cleanse off sweat and cool the body down. In winter they rolled in the snow.

The thermal areas in Iceland opened up new possibilities for the Vikings. They utilized the hot springs as a continuous source of steam by building lodges on top of them. Every time a spring erupted, the steam filled the lodge and the Vikings enjoyed their natural steam bath. The Vikings also bathed in thermal pools that were formed by the hand of nature. Shamans used the steam baths or sweat lodges to cleanse those who were ailing. Tree branches were used to 'beat' around the body of the ailing persons when they came out of the lodge, and thus cleanse their auric field and rid the body of the energy blocks that caused the illness.

The Positive Application:

The Sweat Lodge represents Cleansing at every level of your life. If the mist of the steam is passing over your spread today, it is an indication that you need some form of Cleansing. The Cleansing may apply to any aspect of your life. You may need to Clean out and revalue the company you are keeping. Or you may need to Clean out your home, honor your need to Clean out the old and get things into order in your closets and drawers, or Clean up your financial affairs. But the Cleansing of the Sweat Lodge applies above all to your body and your mind.

Your body is the foundation for your spiritual growth. It is the temple of the soul and needs to be Clean and spotless. That is what your mind must also be. The only way you can experience your connection with the Divine is through your body. But in order to do so, you must learn how to use and communicate with that body. It needs attention and rest, so it can work with vigor. You not only need to nourish the physical body, but also the emotional, the mental and the spiritual bodies. By Cleansing yourself and attending to all your needs, you become a successful Spiritual Viking in the world of today.

The Negative Application:

The mist from the steam in the Sweat Lodge fills your senses, so that you get lost. You are unable to see where and why you need to Cleanse. The mist allows you to become full of self-deception, feeling you are doing so much for yourself and your personal growth. In reality, you aren't doing a thing. But the mist of the Sweat Lodge allows you to maintain your deception. You need to step out of the steam so you can clearly see where you need to let go and allow things to evaporate out of your life. Rejoice in the freedom that follows a good Cleansing. As you Clean out one aspect of your life, you make room for something new to come in. Thus you grow.

CARD 18

THE DRINKING HORN

JOY

18

THE DRINKING HORN - JOY

The Vikings used various occasions of joy and sorrow to lift their Drinking Horns. Every time there was a celebration or a feast, they served mead and drank it from their horns. Weddings and funerals (wakes) called for mead and the Drinking Horn, and so did great victories or successful plunders. The poets set a high value on mead and associated it with their poetic skills, maintaining that they composed poetry on a grander scale if they had the Drinking Horn close at hand. Everyone wanted to relate their use of mead to joy; but sometimes the joy evaporated, and people became drunk and lost control completely, making fools of themselves and at times hurting or even killing people in their stupor.

THE POSITIVE APPLICATION:

The Drinking Horn represents Joy and a reason to celebrate. If the Drinking Horn is in your spread today, it sends you a message of Joy. You have a reason to celebrate some event in your life, either right now or in the very near future. Your relationship with others may have reached a new stage, you have been successful at work or at play, or you may have taken an important step forward on your path of spiritual growth. It serves you best to be moderate in your celebration. Although the Vikings always held the Drinking Horn high when celebrating, there is no need for you to do the same. Only keep in mind that you have a reason to be happy. Joy is the positive force in your life, and the more often you find a reason to be happy and fill your life with Joy, the more fulfillment you enjoy. The ideal is to find a reason for happiness and Joy every day by taking in the simple pleasures of life. Finding Joy in your everyday life, in looking at a beautiful flower, watching the birds fly, or receiving an unexpected smile from a stranger, are all things that call for happiness. Being able to help others also brings you Joy. Life calls for happiness, which is a constant form of celebration if you see the Joy it brings you every moment.

THE NEGATIVE APPLICATION:

You are inclined to raise the Drinking Horn at all times, using it as an excuse for all kinds of celebrations. This urge reflects your avoidance of facing the problems you need to resolve. You fail to distinguish between celebrating and drowning yourself in the self-pity of the Drinking Horn. Another negative application of the Drinking Horn is that you renounce every occasion you have to be happy and joyful. Happiness eludes you, and you look upon Joy as a childish feeling, thus forsaking the important process of personal rejuvenation. By changing your way of thinking, you can open up to Joy and happiness in your life.

CARD 19

MJÖLNIR

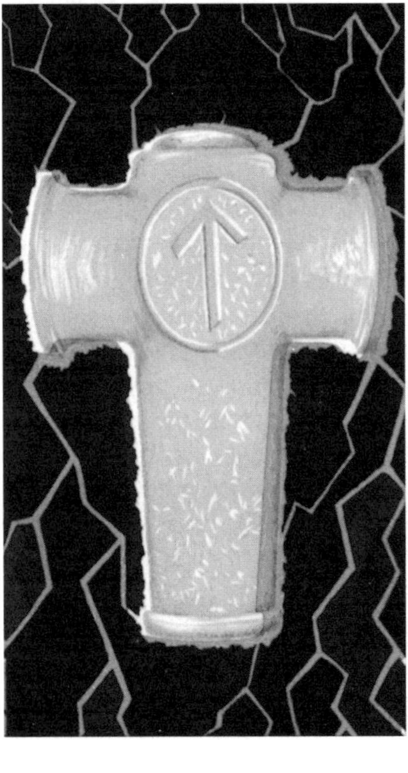

AWARENESS

19

MJÖLNIR - AWARENESS

In the pagan mythology there is a story in which *Loki* (one of the Gods) wagers his head with a dwarf by the name of *Brokkur,* that his brother *Sindri* could not create for him three prestigious objects. The dwarf Sindri accepted the wager and three times he asked his brother Brokkur to blow into the hearth. Each time, Sindri placed a new material on the fire: first a pigskin, then gold, and finally iron. At the first attempt he created *Gullinbursti,* a boar with a brush of gold; at the second, he created a golden ring named *Draupnir;* and at the third attempt he created a hammer named *Mjölnir.*

When these prestigious objects had been created, Brokkur took Loki to *Ásgardur* (residence of the Gods) to have the wager settled. At Ásgardur the objects were given to the Gods. Freyr received the brush, Gullinbursti; Ódinn, the ring Draupnir; and Thor, the hammer Mjölnir. Mjölnir had many outstanding qualities, and could hit everything as hard as Thor desired. Mjölnir could not fail, nor did it miss anything which Thor aimed it toward. Never did it go so far away from its owner that it did not return back into his hand, and the hammer could become small enough to fit into one's pocket, should that be desired. When Thor rode his chariot across the heavens, the hooves of his goats created thunder, and the hammer Mjölnir created lightning. With Mjölnir in his hand, Thor became the guardian of the Gods. The hammer Mjölnir, this remarkable weapon of Thor, was not only used in warfare and to protect the Gods, it was also a sacred symbol used to sanction ceremonies and homes.

THE POSITIVE APPLICATION:

Mjölnir represents the Awareness of the mind, the new ideas and illumination you experience as you enter the inner world. If Mjölnir has struck your spread today with its lightning, its strike creates added Awareness. Ideas may strike your mind like electrified lightning and it is up to you to catch them, process them and manifest them in material ways. If you don't make use of your ideas, they will return to the Universal Mind and be passed on to others. The first step toward manifesting a new idea is often saying it out loud or writing it down. By doing this, you move the idea one step closer to becoming a reality in your life. With its lightning, Mjölnir also proclaims changes in your consciousness. When you work in the inner worlds, your mind constantly reaches new levels of Awareness, which can be referred to as stages of illumination. Thus, you reach higher levels of consciousness. Whenever Mjölnir is around, it lights up your mind and moves you to a new level of Awareness, whether it be in your logical mind or on the intuitive level. Lightning clears the air, helps you get rid of the old, and creates conditions for a greater expansion of your Awareness.

THE NEGATIVE APPLICATION:

You feel that the lightning of Mjölnir comes on too fast, and although you often get brilliant ideas, you have a hard time organizing them and manifesting them in your life. In some cases you start working with your ideas, but spend too much time considering what to do or just talking about them. In neither case are you able to make anything of them. You are stuck in the *"I am going to do..."* pattern. It is the swing of Mjölnir that creates the lightning, but the swing is only the preparation for the throw itself. You must dare to let go of Mjölnir so you will be able to strike your target. If you do not let go of your ideas so that they can reach their target, then they are continuously on the swing and never become a reality. Mjölnir also invokes fear in you toward added Awareness and the illumination of the mind, and causes you to be hesitant in exploring the inner realms of reality.

CARD 20

SLEIPNIR

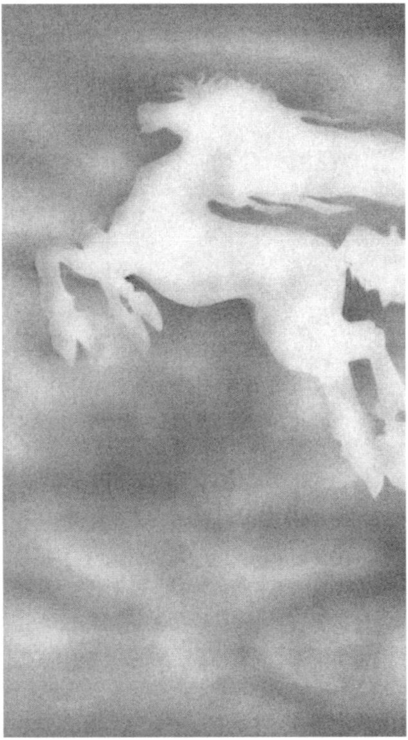

CHANGES

20

SLEIPNIR - CHANGES

The mythology of *Sleipnir,* the eight-legged horse of Ódinn, is very mystical. Nowhere is Sleipnir's role clearly explained. Perhaps his role is best described in *Snorri's Edda*, where Sleipnir is said to represent the wind which enabled Ódinn to travel interdimensionally and visit the dead. Ódinn's riding on Sleipnir is not restricted to the Earth plane or the underworld. He also travels to the heavens, but for the ascension Sleipnir must be able to push himself off from something. The pagan mythology tells of a place where such an ascension occurred. Sleipnir pushed his foot so hard against the Earth in the northeast part of Iceland that he left a large hoofprint there. After Ódinn took off on Sleipnir, the Gods claimed the hoofprint and named it *Ásbyrgi* (the shelter of the Gods). Since then, that hoofprint has been one of the wonders of Iceland.

The Positive Application:

Sleipnir represents Changes in your life. If Sleipnir has galloped into your spread today, he carries with him the fresh winds of Change. Where Sleipnir gallops, trade winds do not reign any more than in Iceland, and the constant alteration of the wind is a good example of the extreme variability of life. The Changes in your life can be mild and effortless, like the spring breeze that caresses your cheeks. They can also be sudden, like when a storm strikes; but keep in mind that when it subsides everything becomes calm, and therefore you need not despair that things will not calm down in your life. The Changes may be like the strong summer winds that blow across Iceland's interior and stir up a lot of dust, so that even the Sun is overshadowed and one cannot see clearly. But such winds also subside. Sleipnir tells you not to fight the Changes, but to jump on his back and ride the winds of Change. Your extended adaptability toward all kinds of Changes makes the process of growth as a Spiritual Viking easier.

The Negative Application:

The Changes that Sleipnir represents cause you anxiety and you feel safer holding on to things as they are. You are repelled by having to follow the natural flow of life. You accept the fact that other people's lives Change, only if yours is allowed to be at a standstill. You feel comforted by the passiveness of the moment and expect growth to come to you without a struggle. Neither airplanes nor birds can fly without resistance. Therefore, resistance creates the best opportunity for you to grow. When you face up to resistance you put yourself to the test, and it is through that test that you grow. Seeking, you find solutions you didn't know were available. Look around yourself, only to see that nothing is at a standstill. Everything is subject to Change. Therefore, you need to overcome your fear of Change.

CARD 21

THE VÖLVA

THE UNKNOWN

21

THE VÖLVA - THE UNKNOWN

The *Völva* was the oracle of the Vikings. With her shamanic powers, she connected with the past and gazed into the future. She was able to foresee things yet to happen, such as success or failure in warfare, people's good fortune in marriage or other relationships, and even the destiny of the Gods themselves. Each Völva used her own method in her shamanic practice. Some journeyed to the inner worlds (upper, middle and lower), and upon returning related what they had learned. Others fell into a trance and channeled their information. Yet others sang themselves (or were aided by singers) into an altered state of consciousness and sought guidance. At times the Völva boiled a *seid* (magic broth), which was magnified by a chanted rhyme. And at other times the Völva used *völubein* (knuckle bones), which she carried in a skin pouch at her belt, threw on a floor or a table, and read the information they revealed according to how they fell. Both Gods and men sought prophecies from the Völva, and she was a prominent person in the communities of the Vikings.

The Positive Application:

The Völva represents the Unknown, your wish to know something that is not evident. If the Völva has chanted her way into your spread today, it is an indication that you are looking for information from the past or a prediction of the future. The presence of the Völva symbolizes that a transformation will soon take place in your life, but the transformation does not always come in the form you expect. It also indicates that what you are seeking is a deep hidden aspect, sometimes an aspect you do not accept as being part of you. The Völva has access to her subconscious and intuitive mind. Her messages are not always clear, so you must pull another card from the deck and place it next to the Völva card. That card gives you an indication of what she wants to tell you. The Völva always uses her intuitive mind when looking for news of past or present, and you are encouraged to do the same. Your own intuitive messages bring you the most blessing. The Völva most certainly sees into the future, but her viewpoint is always based on conditions as they are today. Bear in mind that if you desire a different future, you possess the power and free will to change the message the Völva brings you by changing your course of action.

The Negative Application:

You reject everything that is called supernatural and renounce the validity of the Völva's message, even when it is positive and constructive and gives you guidance. The Völva calls for you to believe in the hidden aspects of life, but you only want to believe in tangible things. Take a look around yourself, and see all the things that have never been visible to you before. Your field of vision is usually quite limited and only allows you to see what you are able to comprehend at that time. It can be compared to the field of vision that a beam from a flashlight gives you in a darkened room. If you turn on the lights in the room, the picture changes and becomes larger. The Völva tries to show you the larger picture of life with her prophecy.

CARD 22

THE SHIELD

PROTECTION/BOUNDARIES

22

THE SHIELD - PROTECTION/BOUNDARIES

Few things gave the Vikings more protection while on the warpath than their shields, and therefore they were an important part of their equipment when they went Viking. The shield gave protection against stones, spearheads, arrowheads and the sharp points of swords and knives. The shield also diminished the effects of blows, and because of the protection it provided, men suffered fewer injuries when attacked. Sometimes while in a battle, the Vikings formed a wall of shields (a wall of protection). Men waited calmly behind it, ready to face the enemy and meet their destiny. The Vikings carved runes on their shields and dedicated them to certain Gods to enhance their protective powers. The shield was the Viking's outer limit, his boundary, and no one could get behind it without meeting opposition. But the Vikings also knew how to let their shields down when that was appropriate, and enjoy life in a carefree manner.

THE POSITIVE APPLICATION:

The Shield represents Protection and your outer Boundaries. If the Shield has been lifted into your spread today, it is here to teach you about your Boundaries and how you can learn to Protect yourself. You are entitled to a sacred space around your body, a space that is under your authority.

Many people have learned to form and respect their outer Boundaries, and claimed their space inside them. If you have no outer Boundaries and are inclined to have people violate your privacy, you need to pull out the Shield and Protect yourself. The Shield is not here to hide behind so that no one can reach you, but rather to provide you as an individual with a natural Protection in your environment. It is up to you to teach others how to respect your Boundaries. It is also up to you to decide whom you allow to enter your sacred space, a space you can imagine consisting of your auric field (hold your arms out from your sides and use them as a measure for the width of the field). Learn to say "yes" when appropriate, and "no" when your heart says so. If you examine your mind and listen to your heart, only to discover that your answer to a certain question is not yes, then it is definitely no. Concepts like "maybe," "later" or "perhaps" are really only substitutes for a "no."

The Negative Application:

You forget that the Shield is part of your Protection. You are unaware of your outer Boundaries, because you have never been taught that you have any and you are used to having people trample on you. You need to lift the Shield up and learn how to apply it. While in the process of learning, one of the most effective applications of the shield is to say "no," and not give in to other people's pressure and continue to do things only to please them. This learning process takes time and you will probably make mistakes, but what matters here, like everywhere else in life, is to have endurance and not give up. Practice makes perfect.

The Shield can also be overused in such a manner that you hide yourself so thoroughly behind your outer

Boundaries that you never dare let the Shield down. By doing so your Protection works in reverse. You become a prisoner behind your own Boundaries, and lose the chance of becoming an active participant in the life that goes on around you.

CARD 23

THE SWORD

RELEASE

23
THE SWORD - RELEASE

No Viking went Viking without his sword by his side. It was necessary to be prepared for attacks from any direction, as the Vikings often sailed through enemy territory. Many of the Vikings were violent, and when they plundered, people were often at the mercy of their swords. According to accounts from the pagan belief, men usually chose to die heroically in battle, because only those who were slain in battle could enter *Valhöll* to live with Ódinn. But in spite of splendid promises of daily battles and festivities at Valhöll, the Vikings held out with their swords as long as they could anytime they had to use them.

THE POSITIVE APPLICATION:

The Sword represents the Release of all things; in this case it is the Release you feel when you gather up enough courage to cut the knots you have created in your own life. If the Sword's point is in your spread today, it is indicating your need for Release. The knots you have created may be of many sorts. Your stubbornness and defiance can hold you back and you may need to cut those knots to gain the flexibility needed for Release. You may need to let go of old habits to get a feeling of Release. Fear and anxiety can be the cause of the knots, and so can being judgmental and prejudiced. You are now presented with an opportunity to cut all these knots, and at the same time Release yourself and others. Release does not suggest that you are getting rid of people or things in your life, only that you are undoing your knots, thereby allowing yourself and others to enjoy the Release and the opportunity it gives you to look at things from a different perspective.

The Negative Application:

The Sword makes demands of Release you do not dare meet. Although you may be a prisoner of your own circumstances, your fear is so great that you hold on to what you know rather than cutting the knots, Releasing yourself and making changes. The negative application of the Sword also shows you that you completely lack flexibility. Gather up enough courage to pull out the Sword and cut the knots to Release yourself. As soon as you sense the inner freedom that Release brings, your life will brighten up and new solutions will be found.

CARD 24

THE STONE OF THOR

SACRIFICE

24

THE STONE OF THOR - SACRIFICE

There are not many known Stones of Thor in Iceland today. One of them is at Thorsnes by *Stykkishólmur;* Thorsnes was one of the first council sites in Iceland. It is very likely that there were Thor's stones at other council places, although there is no evidence or knowledge of them now. Thor's Stone was raised within the circle of judgment at council places, and convicts were sentenced to be sacrificed on it. That was most likely done to make peace with the Gods and to pay for the sins of the convict. It was said that men were *brotnir* over the stone; that is, placed over it either with their back or abdomen facing upwards and thus executed or sacrificed.

THE POSITIVE APPLICATION:

The Stone of Thor represents Sacrifice in some form. If Thor's Stone has settled in your spread today, it is showing you that you need to Sacrifice something. Without being fully aware of it, you are constantly Sacrificing something in your life by choosing to do one thing rather than another. Some Sacrifices are small, others are big. Every Sacrifice has to be made with an open heart to be of any value. Your Sacrifice can be spending time with your child, a friend or a parent, instead of doing something for yourself. Whatever the Sacrifice is, it always needs to be made with a positive attitude, because otherwise you poison the atmosphere around you and ruin the moment both for yourself and others. Sometimes you Sacrifice an old habit for a new one, or an old attitude for a new one, and such Sacrifices usually lead to an increased personal growth. Take a look at where you are making Sacrifices and see if they are leading to greater personal growth. Once you start making Sacrifices with a positive attitude, you will notice the Sacrifices others are making for you.

THE NEGATIVE APPLICATION:

The Stone of Thor is a reminder of how reluctant you are to make any Sacrifices, especially if they are to be made for others. You expect others to make Sacrifices for you, but fail to understand that in a relationship of any kind, people often need to Sacrifice alternately one for the other. The negative application of the Stone of Thor can also be that you accept the role of the victim by constantly Sacrificing yourself for everyone around you, and then end up being hurt and disappointed as no one makes a Sacrifice for you. Then your Sacrifices have exceeded any normal limits. Try to find a balance in your Sacrifices.

CARD 25

THE NORNS OF FATE

DESTINY

25

THE NORNS OF FATE - DESTINY

In the pagan belief, the Norns of Fate were three sisters: *Urdur,* who represented the past; *Verdandi,* who represented the present; and *Skuld,* who represented the future. They sat under the most sacred tree of Ásgardur (*Æsir* were the family of Gods, and *Gardur* meant the home of the Gods), the yew Yggdrasill. Yggdrasill was the tree of life and stood by *Urdarbrunnur* (the fountain of Urdur). The Norns made sure that the tree was always watered. The sisters had strong shamanic powers. Sometimes they journeyed in the shape of swans, making use of the skins of the three swans which swam on Urdarbrunnur. The Vikings believed that the Norns of Fate were present at the birth of every child, and at that time created the child's destiny which could not be changed. Some children were allotted a harsh destiny, while others were favored by the Norns and lived successful lives.

THE POSITIVE APPLICATION:

The Norns of Fate represent your own Destiny and free will. If the Norns have woven their web of Fate into your spread today, they are giving you an indication that you create your own Destiny. Take a close look at the card, and you see that Urdur looks back to the past; Verdandi looks straight ahead at you; and Skuld, the youngest one, looks into the future. The future is like an unwritten page, a story you can write, if you gather the courage. By creating an image of what you want your future to be like and then using your power to work your way from the present into that future, you create your own Destiny. Urdur has grown old. Give her permission to die, but keep the good memories of her. Verdandi is you today, and Skuld is the future you can create. Allow your future to become magnificent and filled with expanded personal growth, compassion and love. Have the courage to walk forward into your future and create your own Destiny.

The Negative Application:

You are stuck in the web of Fate that the Norns have woven for you, enchained in a belief system that tells you that your Destiny cannot be changed. The past, represented by Urdur, holds you in its claws, and her old age and petrified way of thinking keep you bewitched. Your entire life revolves around your past, and because of that you walk backwards into your future. You need to release the burden of your past, deal with it and gather up enough courage to turn around and walk forward with your head high into a future that you are empowered to create for yourself. By doing so you create your own Destiny.

CARD 26

THE SAGAS

KNOWLEDGE

26

THE SAGAS - KNOWLEDGE

One of the most valuable aspects of Iceland's cultural heritage is to be found in all the old manuscripts of the *Sagas* that have been preserved since the 12th century. While other nations in the northern hemisphere lived in the darkness of medieval ignorance and religious fanaticism, people up in Iceland were writing the Icelandic Sagas, and also the Sagas of kings and heroes of other nations. The manuscripts of the Sagas were written on calfskin with ink made from herbs, mainly bearberry bush. Many calfskins were needed for each book. Historical manuscripts of the Sagas include *Snorra-Edda, Heimskringla, Konungsbók Eddukvæda* and *Flateyjarbók.* In the Sagas one finds the only written documentation there is of the old pagan belief that was sacred to the Vikings. The Sagas are therefore of great value, not only to those who live in Iceland, but to the whole world.

THE POSITIVE APPLICATION:

The Sagas represent Knowledge, either new Knowledge that you acquire or Knowledge that is passed down through the generations. If the Sagas have opened up their manuscript in your spread today, they are directing your attention toward Knowledge. It may be time to wipe the dust off some old Knowledge and use it again. Our need for originality at all times has caused us to dispose of valid Knowledge for no apparent reason. The Vikings, for example, knew how to use the Icelandic herbs for healing and invigoration, and that Knowledge was passed down through the generations. But somewhere along the line people stopped learning or passing the Knowledge on, and finally it was all but forgotten, with only a few retaining the Knowledge. Now people all over the world are again turning to herbology, realizing that the cure for almost all ailments is to be found in nature.

You may not need to go as far back as Viking times to find and reinstate Knowledge that is of use to you and that complements other things about which you are Knowledgeable. The Sagas also teach you to have more respect for your own Knowledge, even though it may not have been acquired through academic education. Not all Knowledge comes from books, and we must respect things we learn through other means. Listening to those who are older is a good way to acquire Knowledge. As you obtain more Knowledge and start respecting what you know, your own fountain of wisdom will be the place in which you seek Knowledge.

THE NEGATIVE APPLICATION:

The Sagas show you how you underestimate your own Knowledge. You have a unique Knowledge that no one else has, and you must learn to appreciate your uniqueness as such. You have a tendency to overlook your own Knowledge, and continuously search for something new elsewhere where you think things will be easier and better. In your delusion you think someone exists who can teach you everything at once; but you fail to realize that learning is a process in which you constantly acquire more and more Knowledge. With this attitude, you start believing that things that come from others are better, and totally underestimate your own Knowledge. This is something you need to change, because as you learn to appreciate what you know, you also learn to appreciate who you are.

CARD 27

BLOOD BROTHERS

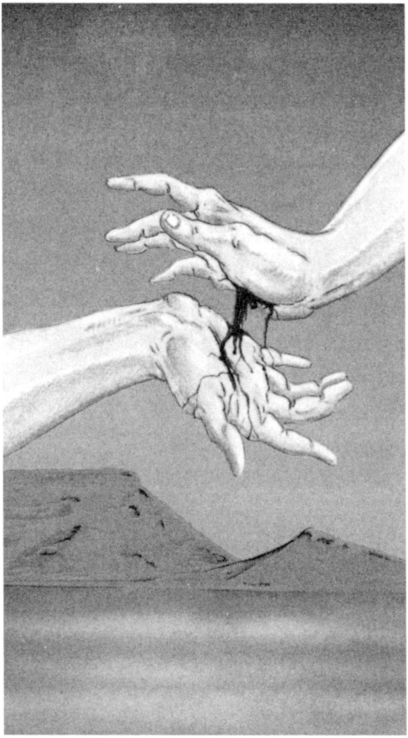

LOYALTY

27

THE BLOOD BROTHERS - LOYALTY

It was customary among the Vikings to become Blood Brothers, and that brotherhood could include more than two men. The Blood Brotherhood was built on the foundation that men would act toward each other as if they were true Blood Brothers born of the same mother. When men became Blood Brothers, they formed lifelong ties of loyalty. If they lived close to each other, they supported each other in everyday life, traveled together and fought side by side. If one Brother was slain by an adversary, the other(s) took revenge. Blood Brothers remained friends and companions through thick and thin, but if one saved the life of the other or did him too big a favor, the other sometimes spent the rest of his life trying to repay the favor, at times without being able to do so. Honor was of great importance to the Vikings; in fact, it was the noblest of all qualities a Viking could have, and each wanted his honor to be flawless. But being honorable also had its drawbacks, for it was difficult for the Vikings to accept a favor (without being able to repay it) even when it came from a Blood Brother.

The ceremony of Blood Brotherhood itself was quite impressive. The Blood Brothers took their oaths in a sense under the Earth. The sides of a long piece of grassy ground were cut up, but left uncut at the ends. The turf was then lifted and propped up in the middle so the Blood Brothers could walk under it. They then turned the soil under the turf, cut their hands and let the blood fall in drops onto it. The soil and the blood were mixed together, symbolizing their connection with Mother Earth. Then the Blood Brothers fell down on their knees and swore an oath of loyalty to each other, calling upon the Gods as witnesses.

The Positive Application:

The Blood Brothers represent Loyalty and helpfulness. If the Blood Brothers have taken their oaths in your spread today, they are here to teach you about Loyalty. Like most of us, you have been taught that Loyalty plays a very important part in every person's life. Being Loyal to one's friends and supporting them is very important. But being Loyal also means you have to be Loyal to yourself. You need to be Loyal to your purpose or goal in life, Loyal to your desires and needs. The Loyalty you have toward yourself is reflected in how you communicate with and relate to others around you. The Blood Brothers are here to show you that you must learn to accept a favor from someone else, without constantly thinking of how to repay it. Permit yourself to accept kindness, love and help from others. The best form of repayment is often obvious gratitude and Loyalty.

The Negative Application:

You feel as if no one shows you Loyalty or kindness. Is it because you are unable to be Loyal to yourself? We usually get back what we give out, and if you aren't Loyal you cannot expect to gain Loyalty from friends. Form a Blood Brotherhood with yourself and use it as a foundation for inner Loyalty. The negative application of the Blood Brothers may also be that you are unable to receive anything from others out of fear of not being able to repay them. You must learn to trust that the Universe will provide you with an opportunity to repay any favor you receive, so you can accept the help offered to you without anxiety.

CARD 28

THE BURIAL MOUND

DEATH AND REBIRTH

28

THE BURIAL MOUND - DEATH AND REBIRTH

At the end of their lives the Vikings were usually buried in a mound. In many places people were put to rest in Viking ships, symbolizing their need for a vessel to undertake the journey across the river between life and death. The deceased were dressed up in their best attire, and on this last journey they often took with them all their treasures, money, food and their favorite horse or dog. In certain cases the slaves of high-ranking individuals were also killed and buried with their masters. It was possibly considered appropriate to bring along your servants when meeting the Gods. Sometimes the ships were burned, but at other times they were just buried in a mound.

THE POSITIVE APPLICATION:

The Burial Mound represents the Death and Rebirth of all things in life, as all things have a beginning, a life span and an end. If the Burial Mound is in your spread today, you are asked to take a look at where you are in the flow of life. Each individual's life is like an endless spiral through which the energy flows, and the same applies to our spiritual growth. Things that worked well for you a couple of years ago have now completed their life span and are at the door of Death. You need to place them in the Burial Mound. Old things need to die, so new ones can be born. The Burial Mound is an indication that such a Death is now necessary in your own life.

To make this turning point as clear as possible, you can actually bury that which is Dead. Get a piece of paper and write down on it everything you are ready to bury from your own life; incidents, memories, emotional hurts or whatever it is that you have worked your way through and is now at the door of Death. Take this piece of paper with you out into nature, along with a shovel and make a small grave. Put all your dead memories into the grave and set fire to them if you so desire. Cover the ashes with soil and create a Mound. End the ceremony by singing a farewell song or rejoice by burning incense that clears away the stagnation of the old energy attached to the things you have just buried. Once the ceremony is over, you will feel a relief within yourself. Turn your face forward and look into a future of great Rebirth.

THE NEGATIVE APPLICATION:

The Burial Mound tells you that you hold on too tightly to things that should long ago have been dead and buried. Your fear to let go of 'dead' things causes your spiritual growth and your life in general to be in complete stagnation. The things you hold on to can be old experiences of pain or conflict, hatred, anger, a 'poor me' attitude, obsessive behavior or overachieving. These experiences can be affecting the health of your physical or mental body, and they really need to 'die' so the flow of life can continue.

Nothing new will happen to you until you dare to let go and allow the Death of an old experience to become the birthplace of a new cycle that brings adventure and new experiences into the life of the Spiritual Viking that you are.

CARD 29

THE MASK

SELF-EXPRESSION

29

THE MASK - SELF-EXPRESSION

The Vikings used the mask both during peacetime and in warfare. In warfare it was used to frighten the enemy, to create within him more fear than the situation called for, and also to protect the face. Thus, the Vikings put on 'another face' when needed. But during peacetime, when they had time to play and amuse themselves, men wore the mask to take on the appearance of either men or animals, while telling great tales of their battles or hunting trips. Thus, the mask served as a form of expression, a tool of transformation of one's own appearance. Masks were also used by shamans. Their masks were sometimes made from the heads or skins of animals or carved out of wood in the form of animals or spirit beings. The shamans used these masks when they sought energy from their power animals, carried out a spiritual healing or journeyed into non-ordinary reality.

THE POSITIVE APPLICATION:

The Mask represents Self-Expression. If the Mask is in your spread today, it is encouraging you to Express yourself and dare to be who you are. You need to drop the Mask you wear every day, and allow yourself to be the person you really are. You have worn many different faces and hidden behind different Masks on your path of life, and have possibly never allowed your true self to appear in front of others. Now is the time to Express your own feelings and thoughts. Seek spiritual strength from within to be yourself in every situation. The Mask also tells you that there are times when you have to reach out for different forms of Expression. Being able to change Masks calls for adaptability. Your Self-Expression must at times differ, depending on which circumstances you find yourself in, but it always needs to ring true to satisfy your inner needs. You need to realize that the Mask is not a hiding place, rather a tool of Self-Expression.

The Negative Application:

The Mask no longer serves as a part of your Self-Expression, but has taken over your face. You have long since stopped realizing that you constantly wear it. You lack the courage to drop the Mask and see yourself as you really are. You find it more important to carry the Mask your surroundings demand than to use Self-Expression. To stand naked in the Light without hiding behind anything demands courage that only the true Spiritual Viking has. Being vulnerable gives you strength, and when you have enough courage to see yourself as you really are, looking at both the good and bad sides without judgment, and accepting who you are, you have won your biggest victory. After that, you can use any Mask you desire if you feel it strengthens your Self-Expression.

CARD 30

THE ARMOR

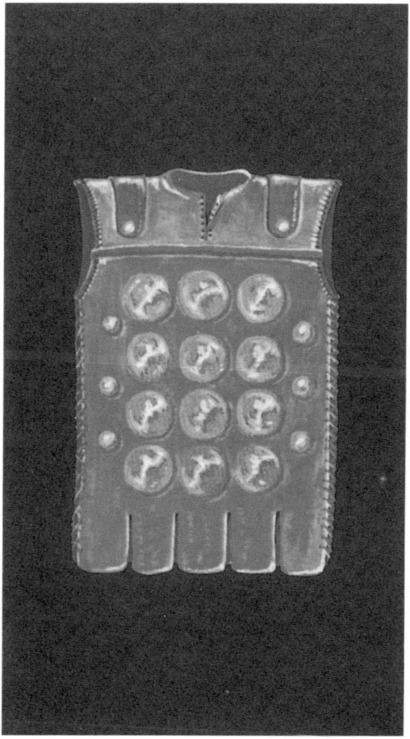

EMOTIONS

30
THE ARMOR - EMOTIONS

Going Viking meant that not only all the arms were taken along on the voyage, but also the Viking's suit of Armor. Only a few Vikings ever owned suits of Armor made from iron, and those who did got them through trade or plunder in the southern part of what we now call Europe. Others had to settle for leather Armor. The suits of Armor were made from thick leather, sometimes of double or triple thickness, that was stitched to increase their protective powers. As the suits of Armor sometimes turned out to be rather thick, the movements of the Vikings were often stiff when they had them on. They were intended to protect the chest, the part of the body where the heart resides.

THE POSITIVE APPLICATION:

The Armor represents your Emotions. Behind the Armor you protect the Emotional centers of your body, the solar plexus (upper abdomen) and your heart chakra (center of chest). The solar plexus is your lower Emotional center, and through it you sense Emotions like self-esteem, courage, boldness, vigor and generosity, or their counterparts such as fear, anxiety, doubt, greed, mistrust, envy and jealousy. The heart chakra is your higher Emotional center, and through it you sense feelings like love, trust, compassion and harmony with all life, or their counterparts. Your task as a Spiritual

Viking is to merge the positive aspects of both Emotional centers and to express them through your open heart.

If the Armor is in your spread today, it is here to guide you in many ways. Most people today have not learned to love themselves enough to feel safe without an Armor. You are no exception, and the Armor teaches you that you need to focus your attention toward yourself and increase your feelings of self-love. Self-love is experienced by acknowledging your own inner power, by letting go of fear, by honoring who you are and honoring your gifts and talents. Each of us was born with the sacred gift of being who we are. By honoring that gift, loving yourself as you are and seeing yourself as a unique individual, you will have no fears of being let down as you will always support yourself emotionally. As you become aware of your inner power and Emotions, you are also able to learn to open your heart up an extra inch every day in the process of learning how to receive life and other peoples' love.

At times it can be necessary to put on the Armor, just as the Vikings did when heading for battle, because every now and then you are faced with forces you do not want too close to you. One of your skills is to learn when to use the Armor and when not.

THE NEGATIVE APPLICATION:

You hide behind the comfort of the Armor and avoid facing your feelings, whether they come from your solar plexus or the center of your heart. You renounce yourself, denying that you must learn to love yourself to be able to love others, and in turn you can suffer from one or all of the following: low self-esteem, fear of lack, greed for love or attention, and envy toward those you feel have more love than you do. Every now and then you connect with others through your heart, but the emotional ecstasy you experience leaves you so full of fear that you immediately hide behind the Armor again. But behind the Armor no one is able to make Emotional contact with you, and you are locked inside like a bird in a cage. You need to let the Armor down so that you can make contact with your Emotions and allow them to flow freely and positively.

As children we are usually willing to experience the world with an open heart. But somewhere along the way we suffer Emotional rejection, and the message we get is that since others do not love us, we cannot love ourselves. This Emotional rejection makes us run to the safety of the Armor, and once there, some of us vow never to open our hearts again. By doing so, we are denying ourselves the right to experience intimacy with others. If we always keep our heart closed behind the Armor, we are neither able to give nor receive. We must be daring enough as Spiritual Vikings to let the Armor fall and start experiencing life through our Emotions. That is the only way we can change our lives and the world we live in.

CARD 31

CURRENCY

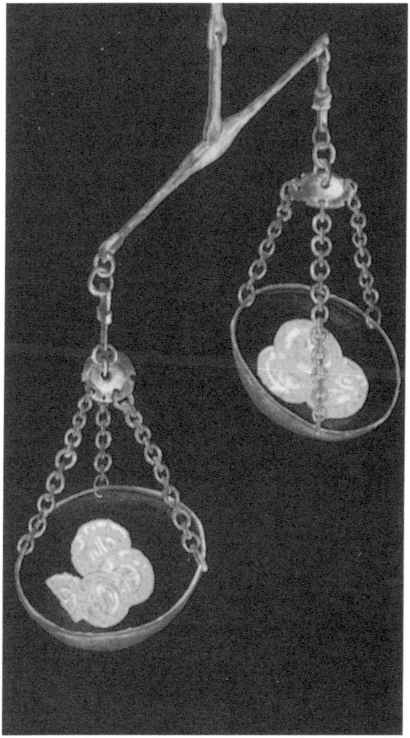

USABLE ENERGY

31
CURRENCY - USABLE ENERGY

The Vikings were great traders, and relics from their towns have revealed various artifacts from different corners of the world. The boldness and courage of the Vikings took them eastward, to the land we now know as Russia, where they traveled along the rivers south to the Black Sea. Westward they sailed to England, Ireland, France and even further west to Vineland, now known as America. Southwards they headed to the Mediterranean, to Greece and Turkey. And to the north they sailed to the Faeroe Islands, Iceland and Greenland. Wherever they went they traded and their range of goods was extensive. The Viking vessels were in a sense the trading fleet of their times, moving goods across the seas or along rivers from one part of the world to the other. Most of the home-based trade towns of the Vikings were in the area we now know as the southern part of Norway and Sweden, and in Denmark. When the Vikings returned from their travels abroad, they traded with the locals and those that visited the trading towns. The currency of the locals was trade goods, such as all kinds of skins, artistically carved walrus teeth, whale bones, and horns. By trading with the Vikings, the locals transported silk, pearls and other luxurious goods farther north. As time went by, people also started using minted coins of silver or gold to pay for their goods. The currency differed, depending on what suited the occasion.

The Positive Application:

The Currency represents the Energy that creates motion. If the Currency has placed its treasures in your spread today, it is bringing you Usable Energy. Whether your Currency today is coins (money) or other valuables, you use both as Energy to move things from one place to another. The Currency does not rule your life, unless you allow it to do so. There is no need to fear the Currency, as it is only a form of Usable Energy. This Energy enables you to make changes in your life and to achieve things. Do not waste your Usable Energy. Use it where you can make the most of it. By looking upon your skills, knowledge and thoughts as Currency, you bring added value to your life. Your ingenuity, your trademark, your drive, and the way in which you get things done all represent Energy that can be used as a Currency in relationships with others. In reality, your own skills are the only Currency of which you are always sure of having enough. Take a look and see whether your friends are willing to exchange Energy with you, or where you can make the most of your own Currency right now. You are never without Currency, if you appreciate who you are and what you know, and use it as Energy.

The Negative Application:

Your ideas about Currency are only associated with money, and you always feel you are in need of more. Because of this attitude, you never feel that you are in charge of any Usable Energy to create movement. You need to create a bank of Usable Energy in your mind, allowing yourself to see how your skills can be used as Currency. Your way of saving can be in the form of exchanging your Usable Energy (skills) for another form of Currency that you can either use or save toward special projects, such as traveling, further education, or play. Whether the Energy you receive is in the form of hard Currency (money) or trade goods, it is always Usable. The Vikings used the long winters to work their skins (and the Scandinavian skins were treasured) or to carve statues or jewelry from the teeth and horns of animals. Gradually, they built up their supply of Currency; by the end of winter they had enough Energy to become owners of pearls, silk and other treasures. You need to move out of your thought pattern of constant lack, and use your own Energy to create.

CARD 32

BIFRÖST

SYNTHESIS

32

BIFRÖST - SYNTHESIS

Between Heaven and Earth the Gods built the bridge *Bifröst* (the trembling road). The humans could see the colors of Bifröst and called it the rainbow, but Bifröst is much safer to travel on than its appearance indicates, and it will not be destroyed until the world comes to an end. The Gods said the red color of Bifröst symbolized the flaming fire that hindered the giants from invading the heavens. Still, the Gods did not need to worry too much about an invasion, because *Heimdallur* stood guard on Bifröst with his *Gjallarhorn* (resounding horn). However, he was only permitted to blow his Gjallarhorn at *Ragnarrök* (the end of the world). But while Bifröst still stood, it was the connecting link between Heaven and Earth, between the material and spiritual world. By traveling along Bifröst, one could enter the spiritual realm and communicate with the spirit world.

THE POSITIVE APPLICATION:

Bifröst represents the Synthesis of all things. Synthesis helps us see the World as one unit, and everyone on Earth as one nation (people), regardless of skin-color, culture or customs. If Bifröst has placed all the colors of the rainbow in your spread today, then you can rejoice because it is an indication that your spiritual growth is moving forward and one stage of it is merging with the next. Next time you see the actual rainbow, take a close look at it. You will notice that it is hard to tell where one color ends and the next begins. The same often applies to your life. When you experience Synthesis on your path of spiritual or personal growth, you are not always aware of it. You often feel you are at a standstill, not making much progress, and it is not until you look back that you realize how far you have gone. Bifröst expresses the importance of your learning to grow into compassion and love, and of your learning to stop separating yourself from those around you. One thing is to say something and another is to do it, but when you learn 'to walk your talk,' then you are working from integrity. Bifröst also teaches you the importance of creating Synthesis between the material and the spiritual worlds in your life. Your body is a manifestation of the Divine in the material world, and when you travel to the spiritual world, you can journey along Bifröst.

The Negative Application:

Your personality has gotten the upper hand, and you are unable to perceive the message of Bifröst about Synthesis. You are afraid you will lose something by giving of yourself. This fear blocks you from seeing that the opposite happens. What you lose is your loneliness, because by Synthesizing with others you comprehend that you are one part of a greater whole, the family of all people. You also learn that as one family you are able to accomplish things that the individual on his own is unable to do. Bifröst also shows you that your seclusion doesn't only apply to your inability to share with others. You are also unable to Synthesize the material and the spiritual planes of your own life. Only your understanding of the need to Synthesize these two planes can make you feel like a whole individual.

SHAMANIC JOURNEYS THROUGH THE VIKING CARDS

The Viking Cards are first and foremost created as cards to help your personal growth and to be used for divination, but the symbols on the cards can also help you on your spiritual journey. The last card in the deck is Bifröst, the bridge between the material and the spiritual world of the pagan believers (*ásatrúarmenn* in Icelandic). Along Bifröst lies the path to the spirit world on which the Spiritual Viking will travel. According to the understanding of the Vikings, your journey along Bifröst takes you to *Ásgardur* (the upper world), but your journeys can also take you to *Midgardur* (the middle world) or *Helheimar* (the underworld), depending on where your shamanic experience and search for certain information takes you in non-ordinary reality.

I wondered for a long time what the Vikings had used for incense at their ceremonies here in Iceland. So I decided to journey to try to find that out. During the journey, I was shown a plant whose name I did not recall. Upon returning from my journey, I pulled out a book on the Icelandic flora, and under the picture of the plant I had been shown was the name *beitilyng* (heather). I have gathered it in the earlier part of summer, before it starts blooming, and dried and burnt it. It gives a pleasant, purifying aroma.

Following are a few guided shamanic journeys you can undertake when you are ready to travel into the inner worlds and go Viking in the non-ordinary realities.

JOURNEY TO MEET YOUR POWER ANIMAL

Shamans of all ages have had powerful guardians from the animal spirit world. Training in nature required forming a strong bond with nature, but the power animals of the shamans did not always have a real model, nor were they necessarily from the shamans' immediate surroundings. They could come from far-away districts, and some of the power animals might, for example, have wings, which they would not have in this reality. As well as providing protection, the animals shared their powers with the shamans when they journeyed into non-ordinary reality or worked on spiritual healing.

Just to give some examples of the power animals of the Gods, Ódinn, the supreme shaman, often journeyed to Helheimar (the lower world) on his horse Sleipnir, who possessed powers of such a nature that he could travel into non-ordinary realities. Ódinn's ravens and wolves were his power animals and sometimes he borrowed the skin of a bird or some other animal during his shamanic journeying. The Norns of Fate under the yew Yggdrasill journeyed in the skins of the swans, and Freyja had her own bird skin.

Those who want to undertake shamanic journeys need to make contact with their own power animal, who then journeys with them, and gives them protection, power and guidance during the journey. It is best to travel along Bifröst to meet your power animal. Your connection to the animal will be stronger if you carry a quartz crystal in your left hand when you set out to meet it.

Choose a quiet place from which to begin your journey. It is good to cleanse the area with incense and light a candle.

If two individuals are working together, one can drum for the other, while the seeker undertakes the journey. The helper can also read the following text for the one who journeys and thus help him through his first one. The helper needs to read the text slowly, so that the one journeying finds it easy to follow. If you are working on your own, you can read the text a few times before your journey and use a drumming tape. It is good to use a drum or some other percussion instrument while journeying because the constant beat of the drum synchronizes the right and left hemispheres of the brain and slows the brain waves down to alpha and theta level. In that state, it is easier for us to enter into other realities.

Place a blanket on the floor to lie on. Take the Bifröst card out of the deck and look closely at it. Think of Bifröst as a bridge between the different levels of reality, between the material and the spiritual worlds. Memorize the rainbow and how its colors create one synthesized unit.

While you journey, you can hold the Bifröst card in your right hand and the quartz crystal in your left hand, which you place on your solar plexus. Tie a bandanna over your eyes. The darkness increases your concentration and helps you to see with your inner vision. Take a few deep breaths. Start by filling your lungs and then your abdomen. When exhaling, first empty your abdomen and then your lungs and sense how your body starts to relax as you let go of all the negative energy that is stored in it. Now you are ready to start your tape or tell your helper to start drumming.

Focus on the top of your head and feel a wave of Light traveling down your body. Sense how deeply you relax when this wave of Light travels through your body. Let it flow calmly and easily down your body, until it reaches your toes and you are completely relaxed. Now focus on your base chakra. Inhale deeply and fill the base chakra with a strong, clear red color. When your base chakra is strong, your feelings of fear, worry and anxiety dissipate, and instead you get feelings of trust, security and fearlessness.

Focus on your second chakra, the spleen chakra. Inhale deeply and fill it with a clear orange color. A strong second chakra drives away boredom, disappointment and frustration, and increases your creative power, discernment and sensuality.

Focus on your third chakra, your solar plexus. Inhale deeply and fill it with a clear yellow color. A strong third chakra drives away feelings of jealousy, anger, contempt, hostility and greed, and makes room for a deeper understanding of your own personal power.

Focus on your fourth chakra, your heart center. Inhale deeply and fill it with green and pink colors intertwined. Have them create a beautiful symphony of colors. Through a strong and powerful heart center, you develop your unconditional love, compassion, friendship and understanding of synthesis. Open up your heart center and learn to receive life through it.

Focus on your fifth chakra, your throat center. Inhale deeply and fill it with a turquoise color. A strong throat center dissipates insecurity and enables you to clearly communicate your feelings and thoughts.

Focus on your sixth chakra, your third eye. Inhale deeply and fill it with an indigo color. A strong third eye dissipates your reservation about other realms of reality and increases your intuitive abilities, allowing you access to your inner world.

Finally, focus on your seventh chakra, your crown center. Inhale deeply and sense how the crown of your head fills with golden and purple colors. Sense how these golden and purple colors expand when you inhale, and radiate from your head when you exhale. A strong crown center amplifies your connection with the Divine and your Higher Self. Little by little, you learn to keep the contact with your Higher Self open at all times, and to move the Light of the Higher Self into your physical body.

Now take all the colors of all your chakras and have them form a rainbow that comes together at your solar plexus. Sense the power of the colors as they synthesize, and see how Bifröst extends from your solar plexus far into the world of spirit. Send out an intent for contact with your power animal.

Focus on the horizon of Bifröst, where you will see a black dot that little by little begins to take form and move toward you. You wait calmly to see what animal is approaching you. As the little dot gets bigger, you begin to distinguish the outlines of an animal and you can tell whether you are being approached by a fish, a creepy crawler, a four-legged animal or a bird. You start seeing the color of the animal and you sense whether it is furry, feathered or scaled. By now you can clearly see your power animal, as it stands directly in front of you. The animal is filled with tenderness and you ask whether it has a message for you.

Listen for the message and memorize it. Invite your power animal to take residence in your quartz crystal and feel how the spirit of the animal settles in it. At the same time, sense how the power of the animal increases your own power. Each animal has something to teach you, but it is up to you to look for that lesson.

Slowly but surely, you withdraw the colors of Bifröst into your quartz crystal. The clear light of the crystal now carries the qualities of all the colors of the rainbow. Put the crystal to your lips and blow your spirit (breath) into it, thus confirming that you and your power animal are now one.

Then send the colors of Bifröst back into each energy center of your body. When you are ready to return, move your body, remove the bandanna from your eyes and sense the reality around you. From now on you can carry your crystal with you. Through it, your power animal is always present. When you set out on an inner journey, always ask your power animal to journey with you.

It is a good idea to write down what you experience on your journeys. Sometimes you do not understand the messages right away, so if you keep a record of them you can look them up when you feel you have reached some understanding.

JOURNEY TO MEET YOUR SPIRITUAL GUIDE

Bifröst represents the synthesis of matter and spirit. When we head into the uncharted territory of our inner world, we are indeed seeking synthesis. Bifröst can be used as a point of entry when you journey toward your spiritual guide.

Start by pulling the Bifröst card from the deck. Choose a place where you will not be disturbed for the next half hour. Cleanse the place with incense and light a candle. If two individuals are working together, one can drum while the other one journeys, but if you are on your own you can use a drumming tape.

Put a blanket on the floor to lie on. Take the Bifröst card and look closely at it, seeing it as the bridge of Light that it is, connecting the material and spiritual world. Memorize the picture of the rainbow, as well as how all the colors form one unit. While you journey you can hold the Bifröst card in your right hand, and if you have undertaken the journey taught in the previous chapter, you can hold your quartz crystal in your left hand and ask your power animal to journey with you.

Tie the bandanna over your eyes. You will be more alert and see more clearly with your inner vision. Take a few deep breaths, and as you exhale, feel how you relax your body and let go of all the negative energy that may be stored up in it. Now you are ready to put on your tape or signal to your helper that he can start drumming. Your helper can also read the journey guide out loud for you.

Focus on the crown of your head, and start sensing a wave of Light that travels down your body. Sense the relaxation that comes with this wave of Light and have it flow slowly over your entire body, until it is filled with Light. Now focus on your energy centers (chakras) one after the other, as you were taught in the guide for the previous journey. When you inhale, you fill the chakras with a clear color. You fill the base chakra with a red color, the spleen chakra with an orange color, the solar plexus with a yellow color, the heart chakra with a combination of green and pink colors, the throat chakra with turquoise color, the brow chakra with an indigo color, and the crown chakra with a combination of purple and golden colors.

Then bring all the colors of the chakras together to form a rainbow that extends from your solar plexus into the world of spirit. With your quartz crystal in your left hand and your power animal by your side, you move out along Bifröst. Somewhere along the way, you feel yourself breaking through a membrane, which is like a thin invisible wall. When that happens, you have entered the spirit world. Soon you will meet your spiritual guide.

Continue your journey along Bifröst, and in the distance you will be aware of someone moving toward you. As you come closer to each other, that being takes on a form, and when you meet you greet each other. This is a Light Being, a master from the spirit world, who is here to help you grow in the material world.

Together you move along Bifröst, surrounded by a clear, bright Light. As you ask your spiritual guide for help, he gives you guidance that will be of use to you in your spiritual and personal growth. Pay close attention to what he tells you and memorize it. You receive the message telepathically. When he has instructed you, he embraces you and tells you that he will continue to watch over you and transmit strength and Light as you continue on your path of growth. You absorb the Love that flows from him and sense how your own Light becomes brighter through the embrace.

As you part, you head back along Bifröst, the colorful rainbow bridge of Light. Slowly but surely, your consciousness returns to your body as each of the colors of Bifröst is drawn into your chakras again. When you are ready to return to this reality, move your body slowly, take the bandanna from your eyes and focus your awareness on your surroundings.

As soon as you have returned from your journey, write down the instructions you received so you won't forget them. Try to use them in your daily life. You will discover that they will be of help. You can journey like this whenever you want to make contact with your spiritual guide and seek advice from him.

JOURNEY TO YOUR PLACE OF POWER

When you journey to non-ordinary realities, your use of the cards is not confined to Bifröst. All the cards can be used as a focus point. I will give you an example. If you need to heal your body, it is good to journey to your Place of Power. As always, it is good to choose a quiet place from which to begin your journey. Cleanse this place with incense and light a candle. If two individuals are working together, one can drum while the other journeys, but if you are working on your own, use a drumming tape. Your helper can guide you through the journey by reading the following text.

Pull the Place of Power card from the deck and memorize the concept 'Place of Power.' Then reflect on which place in nature gives you the most power. Possibly it is a place that you favored as a child, or some beautiful place you have recently discovered. Your Place of Power does not necessarily have to be in your native country. It can be a place you fell in love with while traveling abroad.

When you journey to your Place of Power, you can either choose to sit in a chair or on the floor. Take care that your spinal column is straight and relaxed. Cover your eyes with a bandanna, keep your quartz crystal by your side, and ask your power animal to journey with you. If you prefer not to use a bandanna, you can be in a darkened room, with only a candle lit. Take a few deep breaths and feel how your body relaxes a little more each time you exhale. Turn your tape on or give a sign to your helper that he can start drumming.

Imagine yourself and your power animal in a ball of Light where complete harmony reigns. Keep on breathing evenly and sense how this feeling of harmony slowly fills your body. Your body is completely relaxed, and every muscle and every cell is in complete harmony.

The harmonic vibrations surrounding you are dense and give you support, as you float away in your ball of Light directly to that place in nature you have chosen to visit. You float swiftly, and within moments you have reached your Place of Power. You leave the ball of Light, accompanied by your power animal, and the feeling of harmony keeps on surrounding you.

At some Places of Power, one can find a stone to sit on, at others there is a tussock or some moss, and at yet others there is a grove of trees where you can make yourself comfortable. Sit down in your Place of Power, feeling your power animal by your side, as both of you connect with Mother Earth. Feel how she embraces and receives you. Visualize a narrow cord in some of the colors of the Earth, going from your base chakra down to the center of the Earth. Take a deep breath, and when you exhale, rid the body of all negative energy through this cord. Release all troubles, all negative old memories, all diseases and miseries. Think of the Earth as a recycling plant that receives all this negative energy, recycles it and turns it into positive, usable energy for all.

Put the palm of your right hand on the Earth at the same time as you reach your left arm up above your head and place your palm flat, facing the heavens. Sense how the energy from Mother Earth pours into your body through your right arm, and the Divine energy through the left one. Sense how these two energy fields connect in your body and blend together. Only your body is capable of sensing both the material and the spiritual, and of connecting the two. Feel this connection happening within you and sense how this healing energy travels through your body, thrusting itself into its every cell and filling your body with Light, Love and Energy. It is as if your body is being rejuvenated.

If there is any one part of your body that has been suffering disease, then direct this Energy toward that area and allow it to surround it. Feel how the cells of the body become whole again and start resonating positive energy.

Now you place both the right and left hand on your heart center where you unite the Light and Energy you have just received. At the same time, you affirm that your body now retains both. Then you lie down on the Earth and absorb her Energy through the back of your body, while the front of your body absorbs the warm rays of the Sun.

When you have accepted all the Energy you are able to receive at this point, get up and walk side by side with your power animal slowly toward your ball of Light. You are filled with a new awareness of physical strength after this visit to nature. You are also filled with a sense of lightness and joy as you and your power animal sit down in your ball of Light. Quickly and securely you float back again. You are aware of how the ball of Light envelops your body where you are sitting on your chair or lying on the floor, and slowly you allow the Light around you to be pulled into your heart center. At the same time, absorb the experience you had during this journey to your Place of Power.

When you are ready, move your body and remove the bandanna from your eyes.

JOURNEY TO THE SOLSTICE CAIRN

The card with the Solstice Cairn represents the Light of Life. By working with this card, you can increase the Light in your own life and build a stronger field of Light around you. Through using it, you can also connect with the Spiritual Light.

You can journey (in the outer or inner realms) to any of the Solstice Cairns still intact in Iceland, but if such a journey is not possible, you can then journey to the Solstice Cairn in your cards through the inner planes. Whichever journey you choose to take, you can work in the same way once you reach your destination.

Here I will guide you on a journey through the inner planes. Start by taking a look at the card with the Solstice Cairn. Choose a good spot to journey from. Cleanse the place with incense and light a candle. If two individuals are working together, then one can drum while the other journeys; but if you are on your own, you can use a drumming tape.

You can choose between sitting in a chair, or sitting or lying on the floor. If you sit upright, make sure your spinal column is straight, but at the same time relaxed. It is best not to lean toward the back of the chair you are sitting on, because then the spinal column has to find its own balance, and the energy flow around it will not be restricted. Keep your crystal by your side and ask your power animal to journey with you. Place a bandanna over your eyes and take a few deep and strong breaths, exhaling powerfully. Feel how the energy of the body changes as you change the rhythm of your breathing. Slow down your breathing, but keep on breathing deeply and relax a little more each time you exhale. Start your tape or give your helper a sign he can start drumming.

Focus on the crown of your head and how the golden and purple colors of your crown center amplify with every breath you take, and how they explode with radiance as you exhale. Imagine the golden Light flowing down your body, like a wave of Light. It flows down your head and shoulders, down your arms and torso, over your hips, thighs and legs all the way down to your toes. In your imagination, you are wrapped up in Light. The Light slowly spreads around your body until you are sitting in a ball of Light. In this ball, you and your power animal slowly float away to the Solstice Cairn you have chosen to visit. The journey only takes a few moments, and when you have arrived, you and your power animal disembark from the ball of Light. You take a look at the Solstice Cairn and then walk around it in a circle.

Your walk begins in the East. According to the pagan belief, those who held up the heavens in the four directions were the dwarves Austri (the East), Sudri (the South), Vestri (the West) and Nordri (the North). You sanction your circle by turning your face to the heavens, raising up your right arm and greeting the dwarf Austri: "I greet the East, where the Sun rises every morning and brings Light into my life." Then you continue your walk to the South of the circle, greeting the dwarf Sudri by saying: "I greet the South, where the Light of the Sun shines the brightest and illuminates my path of life." Then you continue your walk to the West, greeting the dwarf Vestri by saying: "I greet the West, where the Sun sets and provides me with an opportunity to focus on introspection." And you walk on to the North, greeting the dwarf Nordri by saying: "I greet the North, where the absence of the Sun teaches me to seek wisdom, gain an overview of my life and let go of the things I no longer need." To complete the circle, you walk on to your starting point.

You turn around, and along with your power animal you walk up to the Solstice Cairn. You find a stone or a tussock by its East side, where you sit down facing the Sun. Look around and enjoy the view you have in every direction. Right in front of you on the ground you will see two beautiful stones. Pick them up, feel them with your hands and take note of their color.

Close your eyes and let the Sun shine on your face. At the same time, start clicking your stones together, so they form a constant beat that synchronizes with the beat of the drum. Suddenly, the Sun seems to burst open, and through the opening flows the Spiritual Light that is behind it. You perceive yourself being bathed in a brighter Light than you have ever experienced, and you also sense that this Light is filled with tenderness. The Light seeks to enter your body through your heart center. From that point of entry, it flows throughout your entire body. It journeys through your cells, muscles, bones, digestive organs and other organs, your endocrine system and your lymphatic system, and takes residence in all the glands of the body. The Spiritual Light illuminates this extraordinary creation that is your body, and when your body is fully illumined you realize how magnificent it is. It is the tool you received as a gift, so that you as a spiritual being could have a human experience.

You are filled with delight and gratitude for having this body, and in your mind you thank it for working as well as it does. You see your body in a new Light, and from now on you will value its work and energy and take better care of it. The Spiritual Light pours into your spinal column and fills it. You are an unlimited being, so you are able to receive as much Light as you want. In your mind's eye you see your spinal column become like a staff of Light that radiates millions of beautiful beams. You sense that you are a channel for the Spiritual Light on Earth. The rays that radiate from you are warm and tender. Your entire circle is filled with this Light.

When you are ready to return, slowly withdraw this Light into your body. Place it in the cells of your body and your spinal column, and it will be distributed evenly to your entire body as you need it. Put the stones into your pocket as you and your power animal get up and walk toward the East out of the circle that you marked for yourself. Then you head for your ball of Light. You and your power animal enter it and flow back into it, until you find that it surrounds your body where you sit or lie. Slowly but surely, you move the Light that now surrounds you into your heart center, and at the same time fill your consciousness with everything you just experienced. Then remove the bandanna from your eyes, open them and adjust yourself to the reality around you.

All the preceding shamanic journeys are only set forth as guidelines. Each and every Spiritual Viking can undertake the journey best suited for him and seek guidance for his own life. The main point is that you continue to journey into the spirit world and add to your spiritual growth. You can always journey on your own, but sometimes it is more powerful if many get together and journey to the drumbeat of one or more of the group.

It is important to realize that the experience of each shamanic journey is individual and is never perceived the same by any two people. Our experiences will therefore not be the same as those of our forefathers the Vikings. Everything is subject to change, and although we are reviving their ways of spiritual practice, our experiences will be subject to our modern-day attitudes and knowledge, and also to the higher vibration of Cosmic Energy that we now have. But we can all reunite with nature through our shamanic practices, obtain protection from our power animals, and receive spiritual guidance that will help us in our everyday life. Therefore I say once again: "May success be yours as you *go Viking* in the inner realms of reality!"

To contact the author, please write:
Gudrun G. Bergmann
Brekkubaer
Hellnum
355 Snaefellsbaer
Iceland

BIBLIOGRAPHY

Some information about the daily and spiritual life of the Vikings has been retrieved from the following books:

Norræn godafrædi, by Ólafur Briem. 6th edition. Publisher: Bókaútgáfan Idunn, Reykjavík 1991.

Heidinn sidur á Íslandi, by Ólafur Briem. 2nd edition. Publisher: Bókaútgáfa menningarsjóds, Reykjavík 1985.

God og hetjur í heidnum sid, by Anders Bæksted translated into Icelandic by Eysteinn Thorvaldsson. Publisher: Bókaútgáfan Örn og Örlygur, Reykjavík 1986.

Víkingarnir, a book created through the coopertion of archaeologists and experts on the Viking Age from various countries. Publisher: Almenna bókafélagid 1967.

Landid, sagan og sögurnar, by Magnús Magnússon. Publisher: Vaka-Helgafell, Reykjavík 1987.

Edda Snorra Sturlusonar, prepared for printing by Gudni Jónsson. Publisher: Íslendingasagnaútgáfan, reissued in 1976.

Heimskringla Snorra Sturlusonar, edited by Bergljót S. Kristjánsdóttir, Bragi Halldórsson, Jón Torfason, Örnólfur Thorsson. Publisher: Mál og Menning, Reykjavík 1991.

Seidur og shamanismi í Íslendingasögunum, by Francois-Xavier Dillmann printed in Skáldskaparmál 2. Publisher: Stafaholt hf., Reykjavík 1992.

The Sacred Triangle of Pagan Iceland, by Einar Pálsson. Publisher: Mímir, Reykjavík 1993.